# Evaluating Viewpoints:
# Critical Thinking in United States History Series

★ ★ ★ ★

BOOK FOUR
## SPANISH-AMERICAN WAR
TO
## VIETNAM WAR

Kevin O'Reilly

★ ★ ★ ★

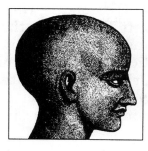

© 1985, 1991
## CRITICAL THINKING BOOKS & SOFTWARE
(formerly Midwest Publications)
P.O. Box 448 • Pacific Grove • CA 93950-0448
www.criticalthinking.com • Phone 800-458-4849 • FAX 831-393-3277
ISBN 0-89455-419-0
Printed in the United States of America

# ABOUT THE AUTHOR

Kevin O'Reilly is a social studies teacher at Hamilton-Wenham Regional High School in Massachusetts. He was named by *Time* magazine and the National Council for the Social Studies as the 1986 Outstanding Social Studies Teacher in the United States. In addition to these four volumes on Critical Thinking in United States History, Mr. O'Reilly is the coauthor of *Critical Viewing: Stimulant to Critical Thinking* (also published by Midwest Publications/Critical Thinking Press & Software) and the author of "Escalation," the computer simulation on the Vietnam War (Kevin O'Reilly, 6 Mason Street, Beverly, MA 01915). Mr. O'Reilly, who has a Master of Arts Degree in History, is an editor of the *New England Journal of History*. He conducts workshops throughout the United States on critical thinking, critical viewing, and decision-making.

> **FOR**
> Mom and Dad and
> Helen and Charlie

# ACKNOWLEDGMENTS

I would like to thank the following for their help: the Hart Nautical Museum at the Massachusetts Institute of Technology for allowing me to make a photocopy of a diagram of the *Lusitania* (Lesson 8); Ron Lovett for his ideas and suggestions on World War I (Lesson 9); Peter Temin, economics professor at the Massachusetts Institute of Technology, for reviewing the interpretations on the causes of the Great Depression (Lesson 14) and explaining some of the more difficult economic problems; Martin Herz for writing a lengthy review of my original lesson on the origins of the Cold War (Lesson 21); Nicole Fasciano, Cathy Luxton, and Garrett Sawyer for their research papers on the Kennedy assassination which helped me write the two interpretations (Lesson 29); and Robert Swartz, professor in the Critical and Creative Thinking Program at the University of Massachusetts at Boston for his suggestions on reasoning, especially cause and effect, and generalizations.

# TABLE OF CONTENTS

# INTRODUCTION

Thinking is what history is all about, as we try to more fully understand our past and thereby ourselves. We don't have many answers in history. Instead, we search for the truth, always attempting to get closer to what really happened. This book is meant to give you a taste of the excitement of historical interpretation and debate. It is also meant to give you guidance in learning the skills necessary to evaluate conflicting viewpoints. The goal is to empower you, as citizens in a democratic society, to make decisions for yourself regarding what you read, see, or hear about the issues of tomorrow—issues where there are few easy answers, and where reasonable people disagree.

This book is about historical interpretations or viewpoints. It is not itself a history book, but rather a series of situations on which historians present differing opinions. The purpose of this book is to teach you how to analyze and evaluate historical arguments.

If you think of a social, political, or economic issue today, you'll realize that people approach problems with different viewpoints. For example, reasonable people disagree about how much money should be spent on social welfare programs, about how to fight crime, and about the best candidate in an election. Historians also disagree about many events in history. Just as there are different ways to tell a fictional story, so there are many ways to tell the story of history. Historians, depending upon their backgrounds and frames of reference, select different information as important or unimportant.

The root word of history is story. As a "story," history seeks to explain past events. Why did a particular event happen when it did? How did a particular person or group of people affect the world around them? What underlying forces shaped events? Good historians have taken the time to step back, to carefully examine events to see the whole picture more clearly, to explain events more fully, and, thereby, to help our understanding of the world.

There are two broad kinds of history: analytical and narrative. In analytical history a historian makes a strong argument about an issue. The thesis is obvious, and the rest of the interpretation consists of a series of arguments to support the thesis. You probably have written thesis/support arguments in your English or social studies classes.

The second kind of history is narrative. Here, the historian tells a story, usually in chronological order. The various elements of the situation—economic forces, technological changes, social institutions, personalities, and so forth—are brought together as the drama unfolds. The main argument or thesis is not always obvious in narrative history. It has to be inferred from the way the story is told. Nevertheless, narrative history also contains a point of view or a thesis about why events happened the way they did.

This book presents both analytical and narrative history. For example, the interpretations on American Imperialism in Lesson 7 are narrative; the interpretations in Lesson 8 are analytical; most are a combination of both.

One of the most important goals of this book is to introduce you to the conflicting viewpoints or interpretations of history. Ideally, you would read the actual books containing the historical interpretations of events, some of which are listed on pages 167–170. Realistically, you don't have the time to read all of these historical works. So this book contains short summaries of the interpretations. In some cases 300-page books have been summarized into one or two pages. Since this isn't fair to the original historians, their names have been replaced by titles: Historian A, Historian B, and so forth.

In some lessons the viewpoints are entitled Interpretation A or Theory A, rather than Historian A. Interpretation or Theory is used when no particular historian is identified with that point of view. These terms are also used to convey the idea that you should be forming your own interpretations or theories. The dictionary defines interpretation as "an explanation of what is not immediately plain or obvious," and it defines theory as "a judgment based on evidence or analysis." Ask your science teacher how the term *theory* is defined in science.

While most arguments presented in this book are those expressed by historians, a few are from historical participants. Thus, there are arguments by Lenin on the economy (Lesson 7) and the Supreme Court justices in *Brown vs. Board of Education* (Lesson 26).

This student book is comprised of three components:
*Guide to Critical Thinking* explains the parts of an argument and how to evaluate those parts.
*Worksheets* provide practice in the skills necessary for evaluating and constructing arguments.
*Historical interpretation problems* provide the opportunity for you to analyze historical arguments and make up your own mind.

Lessons within the book are arranged into four units: World Power (Lessons 1–9), 1920s and the New Deal (Lessons 10–16), Foreign Policy Since 1945 (Lessons 17–22), and Modern American Society and Politics (Lessons 23–29).

Fifteen of the lessons (#1–5, 10–12, 17–19, and 23–26) are short worksheet lessons which focus on practicing particular skills. The other fourteen lessons (#6–9, 13–16, 20–22, and 27–29) are longer historical interpretation problems where the skills can be applied.

# UNIT 1
# GUIDE TO CRITICAL THINKING

**Purpose of This Unit**

This Guide is meant to help you improve your critical thinking skills. Critical thinking, as used in this book, means evaluating or judging arguments. The critical thinker asks, "Why should I believe this?" or "How do I know this is true?" Just as importantly, critical thinking means constructing good arguments. Here, the critical thinker asks, "Why do I believe this?" and "Do I have a logical, well-supported case to back up my claims?"

As mentioned in the Introduction to this text, you are going to be confronted in this book with opposing viewpoints. You will have to decide for yourself which are stronger and which are weaker. This Guide will help you with the critical thinking skills necessary to judge the viewpoints presented and to express your own verbal and written views on topics.

Historians use critical thinking skills constantly in evaluating the reliability of documents, in selecting what is important, and in determining the underlying causes for events. But critical thinking is useful in everyday life as well. It is called for in such situations as buying a car, watching the news, voting, or deciding on a job or career. Improved skills in this area will help you make better judgments more often.

You can get an overall picture of critical thinking by reading through this Guide. You will find it most useful, however, when you need to use a particular skill in a particular lesson. For example, the section on evaluating **Generalizations** will be useful in Lesson 9, which asks several questions on recognizing and drawing good generalizations.

**When Is an Argument Not a Fight?**

An *argument* or interpretation, as used in this Guide, refers to presenting a conclusion and defending it with reasons that logically lead to the conclusion. You will have to decide for yourself how strong each argument is. A *case* is a set of arguments. The strength of a case may be judged by examining individual arguments. Arguments or interpretations may include any or all of the following components.

• Assertions • Evidence • Reasoning •
• Assumptions • Values•

Keep the importance of words in mind as you look through the following pages. Words are the keys to arguments. Signal words like "but," "however," and "on the other hand" indicate a change of direction in an argument. Words will serve as your clues in identifying parts of an argument and, once the argument has been identified, they will serve as your keys in analyzing the strength of that argument.

Once you recognize an argument, you will want to analyze it. You will break it down into its respective parts and evaluate the elements against certain standards of excellence in reasoning and evidence. You will examine the assumptions to see if they are warranted. You will consider how the author's values shape the evidence and reasoning presented.

## Assertions

An assertion is a statement, conclusion, main point, or claim concerning an issue, person, or idea. It can be the conclusion of a very short argument, or it can be the main point (thesis) of an argument of perhaps two or more paragraphs.

For example, consider the short argument, "Bob is very responsible, so I'm sure he'll show up." The conclusion (assertion) in the argument is the phrase "...so I'm sure he'll show up." (The part of the argument that isn't the conclusion ["Bob is very responsible,..."] is called the premise. Premises are assumptions or reasons offered to support a conclusion. See the section on **Assumptions**, pages 15–16.)

### IDENTIFYING ASSERTIONS

Words that often cue an assertion or conclusion include "therefore," "then," "so," and "thus." You can also identify an assertion by asking yourself, "What is the author trying to prove? Of what is the author trying to convince me?"

### EVALUATING ASSERTIONS

Two important questions to ask to evaluate the overall assertion of an argument are:

- Is the assertion supported by good reasons (supporting arguments)?
- Are the reasons supported by evidence?

## Evidence

Evidence consists of the information a person uses to support assertions. It is the data, information, and knowledge which a historian, social scientist, or any communicator uses to support an argument; it is not the argument or interpretation itself.

There are many sources of evidence. Some of the more common sources include statements by witnesses or other people, written documents, objects, photographs, and video recordings. Lack of sources for evidence seriously weakens an argument. That is why many historical works include footnotes to cite sources; that is also why you should cite sources in essays you write.

For example, historians studying a Civil War battle could gather written accounts of the battle from sources such as diaries, battle reports, and letters. They could examine objects that had been found on the battlefield and photographs taken at the time of the battle. They also might use accounts by other historians, but these would be weaker sources because they are not eyewitness accounts (see primary sources below).

IDENTIFYING EVIDENCE

To help locate evidence in an argument, look for endnotes, quotation marks, or such words as "according to," "so-and-so said," or "such-and-such shows."

The initial questions to be asked when evaluating any evidence offered in support of an argument should be:
- Is there a source given for this information?
- If so, what is it?

EVALUATING EVIDENCE

Only when you know the sources of evidence can you judge how reliable the evidence actually is. Frequently, you can use the following evaluation method when considering evidence and its sources. This can be shortened to **PROP**; remember that good sources will "prop up" evidence.

> **P**  Is it a primary (eyewitness) or secondary (not an eyewitness) source?
>
> Primary sources are invariably more desirable. To reach valid conclusions, you need to realize the importance of primary sources and gather as many as possible to use as evidence in an argument. You should depend on secondary sources, like encyclopedias or history texts, only when primary sources are unavailable.
>
> **R**  If the source is a person, does he or she have any reason to distort the evidence?
>
> Would those giving the statement, writing the document, recording the audio (or video), or identifying the object benefit if the truth were distorted, covered up, falsified, sensationalized, or manipulated? Witnesses with no reason to distort the evidence are more desirable than those who might benefit from a particular presentation of the evidence.
>
> **O**  Are there other witnesses, statements, recordings, or evidence which report the same data, information, or knowledge?
>
> Having other evidence verify the initial evidence strengthens the argument.
>
> **P**  Is it a public or private statement?
>
> If the person making the statement of evidence knew or intended that other people should hear it, then it is a public statement. A private statement may be judged more accurate because it was probably said in confidence and is, therefore, more likely to reflect the speaker's true feelings or observations.

These four factors (**PROP**) will be enough to evaluate most evidence you encounter. Additional factors that are sometimes considered regarding evidence include:

*Witnesses*

- What are the frames of reference (points of view) of the witnesses? What are their values? What are their backgrounds?
- Are the witnesses expert (recognized authorities) on what they saw?
- Did the witnesses believe their statements could be checked? (If I believe you can check my story with other witnesses, I am more likely to tell the truth.)
- Was what the witnesses said an observation ("Maria smiled") or an inference ("Maria was happy")? Inferences are judgments that can reveal much about the witnesses' points of view or motives (reasons) for making statements.

*Observation Conditions*

- Were physical conditions conducive to witnessing the event? (Was it foggy? Noisy? Dark?)
- What were the physical locations of the witnesses in relation to the event? Were they close to the action? Was there anything blocking their view?

*Witnesses' Statement or Document*

- Is the document authentic or a forgery?
- What is the reputation of the source containing the document?
- How soon after the event was the statement made?
- Did the witnesses use precise techniques or tools to report or record the event? For example, did they take notes or use reference points?

## Reasoning

Just as evidence can be judged for its reliability, so reasoning can be evaluated for its logic.

Reasoning is the logical process through which a person reaches conclusions. For example, you notice that the car is in the driveway (evidence) so you reason that your mother is home (conclusion). Five kinds of reasoning are frequently used in historical interpretations:

- cause and effect
- comparison
- generalization
- proof (by evidence, example, or authority)
- debating (eliminating alternatives)

These types of reasoning, along with questions to help evaluate them and fallacies (errors in reasoning) for each, are explained below.

## Reasoning by Cause and Effect

This type of reasoning is used when someone argues that something caused, brought about, or will result in something else. For example, Laura's motorcycle will not start (effect), so she decides it must be out of gas (proposed cause).

Causation is very complex—so complex that some historians feel that they do not really understand the causes of an event even after years of study. Other historians do not even use the word cause; instead they talk about change. Please keep a sense of humility when you study causation. When you finish your course, you are not going to know all the causes of complex events. Rather, you are going to know a little bit more about how to sort out causes.

Historians believe in multiple causation, that is, that every event has several or many causes. This belief does not, however, relieve us of the responsibility of trying to figure out which are the most important causes. Indeed, one of the most frequent sources of debate among historians stems from disagreements over the main causes of events.

### IDENTIFYING CAUSE-AND-EFFECT REASONING

One way to identify cause-and-effect reasoning is to watch for such cue words as "caused," "led to," "forced," "because," "brought about," "resulted in," or "reason for." You can also identify it by asking, "Is the author arguing that one thing resulted from another?"

### EVALUATING CAUSE-AND-EFFECT REASONING

Several important questions may be used to evaluate the strength of a causal explanation.

- Is there a **reasonable connection** between the cause and the effect? Does the arguer state the connection?

  In the motorcycle example, for instance, there is a reasonable connection between the motorcycle being out of gas and not starting. Lack of gasoline would cause a motorcycle not to start.

- Might there be **other possible causes** for this effect? Has the arguer eliminated these as possible causes?

  There are also, however, other possible causes for a motorcycle failing to start. Maybe the starter isn't working. Other possible causes have not been eliminated.

- Might there be **important previous causes** that led to the proposed cause?

  In some cases a previous cause might be more important than the proposed cause; e.g., a leak in the gasoline tank might cause a motorcycle to be out of gasoline. In this case simply putting gasoline in the tank will not make the engine run again.

**Cause-and-Effect Fallacies**

*Single cause*

Any conclusion that a historical event had but one cause commits the single-cause fallacy. For example, the statements "Eloise married Jon because he's handsome" and "Antiwar protest caused the United States to pull out of the Vietnam War" both make use of the single-cause fallacy.

In both cases there are likely to be other factors, or causes, involved. The fallacy can be avoided by carefully investigating and explaining the complexity of causes. Be careful, however. Historians may sometimes assert that something "caused" an event when they really mean it was the main, not the only, cause.

*Preceding event as cause*

A Latin phrase (*Post hoc, ergo propter hoc*), meaning "after this, therefore because of this," is the technical name of a fallacy that occurs when someone assumes that because event B happened after event A, A caused B. "I washed my car, so naturally it rained" and "Since the Depression followed the stock market crash of 1929, the stock market crash must have caused it" are both examples of this fallacy. To avoid the error, the author of the argument must explain how A caused B.

*Correlation as cause*

This fallacy occurs when a conclusion is reached that because A and B occurred at the same time or occur regularly at the same time (the correlation), then one caused the other.

Some correlations, such as cigarette smoking and increased incidence of heart disease, are very strong. Others are not as strong. In some correlations where A is argued to cause B, ask yourself if B could instead have caused A. For example, "Students who have fewer absences (A) achieve higher grades in school (B)." In this case, consideration might also be given to the correlation that "Students who achieve higher grades in school (B) have fewer absences (A)."

Again, the fallacy might be avoided by an explanation of how A caused B. Since, however, a connection cannot always be shown, people are frequently forced to rely on correlations. For example, you don't have to know, mechanically, *how* a car works to know that turning the ignition should cause it to start.

*False scenario*

This fallacy uses the argument that if something had happened, then something else would have happened (or if something had not happened, then something else would not have happened). "If you hadn't told Mother on me, I wouldn't be in trouble" is an example of false-scenario reasoning. "If we had not built railroads in the late 1800s, the United States would not have had as much economic growth as it did with the railroads" is another.

Although some of this kind of predicting can occur when we have a great deal of evidence regarding what might have happened, it is generally much less certain than causal reasoning about what actually did happen. To avoid this fallacy, concern yourself with what actually happened rather than what might have happened.

## Reasoning by Comparison

This type of reasoning, sometimes called "reasoning by analogy," consists of two basic types, both of which involve drawing comparisons between two cases.

*Alike comparison*

The first type of comparison chooses two cases (people, events, objects, etc.) and reasons that since they are alike in some ways, they will be alike in some other way. For example, Joe might reason that Fernandez did all his homework and got an "A" in geometry, so if Joe does all of his homework he can also get an "A." Joe is reasoning that since the two cases (his and Fernandez's) are similar in terms of homework (doing it all), they will be similar in terms of outcome (an "A").

*Difference comparison*

The second type compares two cases and reasons that since they are different in some respect, something must be true. For example, Juan might reason that his baseball team is better than Cleon's, since Juan's team won more games. Juan is concluding that since the two cases (teams) are different in some respect (one team won more games), it is true that the team that won the most games is a better team.

If Joe and Fernandez are taking the same course (geometry), and have the same mathematical ability and the same teacher, then the conclusion that the outcome would be the same is stronger than it would be if they were different in any or all of these areas. If the two baseball teams played the same opponents and the same number of games, then the conclusion that one team is better (different) than the other is stronger than it would be if they were different in any of these ways.

Usually, more similarities make a stronger argument. A similarity found in an argument of difference, however, will weaken the argument. If the two baseball teams had the same winning percentage, then the conclusion that one was better (different) than the other would be weakened by this similarity.

As another example of a difference comparison, examine the argument: "The federal budget deficit increased from $800 billion three years ago to $912 billion this year. We've got to do something about it before it destroys our economy." What if the federal budget deficit were 4% of the Gross National

Product (the measure of goods and services produced in a year) three years ago and 4% this year also? Here, a similarity found between the deficits of the two years being compared weakens the conclusion that the federal budget deficit is getting worse. Thus, differences weaken arguments comparing similarities, and similarities weaken arguments comparing differences.

IDENTIFYING
COMPARISON
REASONING

Cue words can help identify comparisons. Watch for such comparative terms as "like," "similar to," "same as," "greater (or less) than," "better (or worse) than," and "increased (or decreased)." Some comparisons, however, are implied rather than stated. For example, someone might say, "Oh, I wouldn't travel by plane. It's too dangerous." You might ask "dangerous compared to what?" If a higher percentage of people are injured or killed using alternate methods of travel (automobiles, trains), then the statement is weakened considerably.

> In examining comparisons, ask yourself:
> • How are the cases similar; how are they different?

EVALUATING
COMPARISON
REASONING

This skill involves *evaluating comparison arguments*. It is not the same activity as "compare and contrast," where you are asked to find the similarities and differences between two items; i.e., "Compare and contrast the American and French Revolutions." In evaluating comparison arguments you, on your own, are to recognize that a comparison argument is being made and, without being told, ask about the similarities and differences of the two cases being compared.

**Reasoning by Generalization**

This kind of reasoning includes both definitional and statistical generalizations. The generalization, "No U.S. senator is under 30 years of age" is an example of a *definitional generalization*, since by legal definition, a United States senator must be at least 30 years of age.

*Statistical generalization* is important to evaluating historical arguments. Statistical generalizations argue that what is true for some (part or sample) of a group (such as wars, women, or songs) will be true in roughly the same way for all of the group. For example, Maribeth might argue that since the bite of pizza she took (sample) is cold, the whole pizza (the whole group) is cold.

Statistical generalizations can be further subdivided into two types. *Hard generalizations* are those applied to all (or none) of the members of a group, e.g., the whole cold pizza above, or a statement like "All the apples have fallen off the tree." A hard generalization is disproved by one counterexample (contrary case). For example, if there is one apple still on the tree, the generalization is disproved.

*Soft generalizations* are those applied to most (or few) members of a group, e.g., "Most people remember the Vietnam War." A soft generalization is not disproved by one—or even several—contrary cases, but the generalization is weakened as the contrary cases add up. For example, if someone says that Luis does not remember the Vietnam War, the generalization is not disproved. If, however, that person cites fifty people who do not remember the Vietnam War, the generalization is getting shaky.

The probability that a statistical generalization is correct increases with the size of the sample and the degree to which a sample is representative of the whole group. Your generalization that "Nella is prompt" is more likely to be accurate if she was on time on all twenty occasions when she was supposed to meet you than if she was on time the only time she was supposed to meet you.

Representativeness is even more important than size in generalizations. In the pizza example the sample is quite small (only one bite from the whole pizza) but very representative—if one part of the pizza is cold, it is highly likely that the whole pizza is cold. Similarly, presidential election polls are small (about 1200 people polled) but usually very accurate, since those sampled are quite representative of the whole electorate. If you think of the whole group of voters as a circle, a presidential election poll might look like Figure 1.

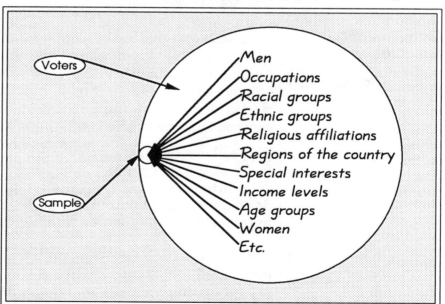

*Figure 1. The sample should represent all these groups of voters (and many more) in the same proportion as they make up the whole electorate.*

IDENTIFYING
GENERALIZATIONS

You can recognize statistical generalizations by watching for their cue words ("all," "none," "some," "most," "a majority," "few") or plural nouns ("women," "farmers," or "people").

EVALUATING
GENERALIZATIONS

Questions you should ask when evaluating generalizations include the following.

> • How large is the sample?
> The strength of a statistical generalization is improved by larger sized sampling.
> • How representative is the sample?
> If you picture the generalization as a little circle and a big circle, as in Figure 1, the question becomes: Does the little circle have all the same subgroups in the same proportion as the big circle?

You should not, however, be concerned only with evaluating generalizations that other people make. You should also be concerned with how far you can legitimately generalize from what you know.

For example, if you learned that slaves on ten large cotton plantations in Maryland in the 1850s were brutally treated, you might generalize that slaves on most large cotton plantations in Maryland at that time were brutally treated. You would be on much shakier ground, however, to generalize that slaves on most plantations were brutally treated at all times. You really have no information about slaves on, say, small Virginia tobacco plantations in the 1720s, so you shouldn't make such a broad generalization. The warning is, "Do not overgeneralize."

## Generalization Fallacies
*Hasty generalization*

This fallacy consists of a general conclusion based on an inappropriately small or unrepresentative sample. For example, suppose a reporter polls three people in Illinois, all of whom say they support gun control. If the reporter concludes that all (or even most) people in Illinois support gun control, then he or she is making a hasty generalization.

This fallacy includes such oversimplifications as "If it weren't for bankers, we wouldn't have wars." To avoid such fallacies, remember that any group (such as people, wars, or depressions) is quite complex and must be carefully sampled to take those complexities into account.

*Composition and division (stereotyping)*

These two related fallacies confuse the characteristics of the group and the characteristics of the individuals within that group. In composition, the characteristics of the individual(s) within the group are ascribed (given) to the whole group. ("She's a good lawyer, so the law firm she is a member of must be a good firm.") In division, characteristics that belong to the group as a whole are assumed to belong to each of the individuals. ("She's a member of a good law firm, so she must be a good lawyer.")

These fallacies are commonly referred to as *stereotyping*, which is defined as "applying preconceived ideas to a group or members of a group." This results in the groups or individuals being judged before we really know them. This act of prejudging is where we derive the word *prejudice*. "You're Jewish, so you must be well educated" and "Of course he's a drinker, he's Irish!" are examples of stereotype statements.

**Special pleading**

In this fallacy the arguer presents a conclusion based on information favorable to the argument while ignoring unfavorable information. ("Mom, I should be able to go to the dance. I passed my history test and got an 'A' in math." [...omitting the information that I failed science and English.]) A good argument avoids this fallacy by including unfavorable information and overcoming it with compelling reasons for accepting the thesis or conclusion.

## Reasoning by Proof (evidence, example, or authority)

These types of reasoning concern whether or not the evidence or authority used supports the point being argued. It does not concern the strengths and weakness of the evidence itself (see the **Evidence** section of the Guide). Similarly, the word "proof" as used here does not mean absolute proof—as in mathematics—but rather refers to methods used to support an argument or interpretation.

This is generally a legitimate method of supporting an argument. For example, a doctor might be called to testify in court to support the argument that a claimant had certain injuries (proof by authority). A biologist might explain the results of several investigations (example), cite evidence gathered (evidence), and quote the written opinions of several experts (authority) to support an argument on the effects of toxic waste.

**IDENTIFYING PROOF REASONING**

Proof reasoning can be identified by cue words such as "for example," "for instance," "according to," "authority," and "expert." When evaluating argument by proof, you should look at the answers to several questions:

**EVALUATING PROOF**

*Evidence*

*Examples*

*Authority*

> • Does the evidence prove the point being argued? Does it support the point under consideration?
>
> • Are the examples pertinent to the argument?
>
> • Is this person an expert on this particular topic? What are the qualifications of the authority? Are they presented?
>
> • Do other authorities agree with these conclusions? Are there any authorities who disagree with the conclusion? Are counterarguments acknowledged and/or refuted?

**Fallacies of Proof**

*Irrelevant proof*

Arguments which present compelling evidence that does not apply to the argument in question are fallacies of irrelevant proof. For example, "If you flunk me, I'll lose my scholarship" and "Everyone else does it" are fallacies of irrelevant proof. As a further example, suppose Senator Smith is accused of taking bribes to vote for certain laws and, in his defense, presents a great deal of evidence that shows he is a good family man. This evidence does not concern his actions as a senator and is thus irrelevant to the charges. Good arguments avoid this fallacy by sticking to the issue under question.

*Negative proof*

This fallacy type presents a conclusion based on the lack or absence of evidence to the contrary. For example, "There is no evidence that Senator Macklem is an honest woman, so it's obvious she is a crook" or "Since you haven't proven that there is no Santa Claus, there must be one." Remember that you must present evidence to **support** your conclusions when you are making a case.

*Prevalent proof*

Related to the fallacy of negative proof, this fallacy concludes that something must be the case because "everyone knows" it is the case. Such arguments as "Everyone knows she's a winner" and "Politicians can't be trusted; everyone knows that" are examples of the prevalent proof fallacy. Remember, in previous times "everyone knew" that the sun revolved around the earth! The critical thinker sometimes asks questions even about things which everyone knows.

*Numbers*

A conclusion that the argument is right solely because of the great amount of evidence gathered commits the fallacy of numbers. For example, "We checked hundreds of thousands of government records, so our theory must be right."

Notice that no mention is made of what the "government records" contained—the argument only states that they were "checked." A great deal of evidence can be amassed to support a slanted perspective or an argument using poor reasoning or faulty assumptions. When constructing arguments, check them not only for strong evidence but also for sound reasoning and assumptions.

*Appeal to authority*

A conclusion that is based only on the statement of an expert commits the appeal-to-authority fallacy. Such arguments conclude, "I'm right because I'm an expert" and lack additional supporting evidence. For example, the argument "It must be true because it says so right here in the book" is based only on the "authority" of the book's author. Arguments must be judged on the strength of their evidence and their reasoning rather than solely on the authority of their authors.

*Appeal to the golden mean*

This logical fallacy is committed when the argument is made that the conclusion is right because it is moderate (between the extreme views). If someone argued, "Some people say Adolf Hitler was right in what he did, while others say he was one of the most evil leaders in history. These views are so extreme that a more moderate view must be right. He must have been an average leader," he or she would be appealing to the golden mean. (Of course, the "extreme" view that Hitler was evil is right in this case.)

This fallacy can be avoided by realizing that there is no reason for an extreme view to be wrong simply because it is extreme. At one time it was considered "extreme" to think that women should vote or that people would fly.

## Reasoning by Debate (eliminating alternatives)

Reasoning by debate helps a person see why one interpretation should be believed over other interpretations and puts an interpretation into a context. It is not surprising, therefore, that articles in historical journals frequently begin by a survey of other interpretations of the topic under study and an attempt to refute opposing interpretations.

This type of reasoning advances an argument by referring to and attempting to show the weaknesses of alternative interpretations. This attempt to disprove, called debating, is not only acceptable, but desirable. For example, someone might argue, "Peter thinks Mi-Ling will get the lead role in the play, but he's wrong. Lucetta has a better voice and more acting experience, so she'll get the lead." A historian might argue, "Although the traditional view is that slavery is the main cause of the Civil War, people who hold that view are wrong. Economic problems, especially over the tariff, were the main cause of the bloody war." Both are applying reasoning by debate.

IDENTIFYING DEBATES

Cue words for this type of reasoning include "other people believe," "the traditional view is," "other views are wrong because," "older interpretations," and "other viewpoints are."

EVALUATING DEBATES

To help evaluate debate reasoning, ask questions like the following.

> • Have all reasonable alternatives been considered? Have they all been eliminated as possibilities?
> • Does this author attack the other views in a fair way?
> • What might the authors of the other views say in response to this argument?

In eliminating possible alternatives, the author must be careful to attack the argument rather than the arguer, to present reasoned evidence against the argument, and to fairly interpret the alternative argument under consideration. This form of questioning can also be helpful when there is a lack of information.

**Fallacies of Debate**

*Either-or*

This fallacy presents a conclusion that since A and B were the only possible explanations—and since A was not possible, B is proven to be the explanation. For example, "Only Willis and Cross were around, but Willis was swimming so Cross must have done it." What if someone else was actually around but no one saw him or her?

Of course, eliminating alternatives can be very important to reasoning a problem through, as Sherlock Holmes demonstrates so well. But one must be careful to ask: Have all alternatives been eliminated? Could it be both alternatives? Don't let yourself be "boxed in" by this type of reasoning.

*Attacking the arguer*

(In logical terminology, this is called *ad hominem*—Latin for "to the man.") This fallacy occurs when statements are directed at the person making the argument rather than at the arguments presented. For example, the statement "No one should listen to what Mrs. Rouge says. She's a Communist" is an attack on Mrs. Rouge personally rather than on the statement she made.

Sometimes the attack is more subtle, such as a look of disgust, a negative comment ("I don't believe you just said that"), or sarcastic laughter. Good arguments avoid this fallacy by refuting the argument, not the person.

*Straw man*

This is the technique of attacking the opponents' argument by adding to or changing what a person said, then attacking the additions or changes. For example, Johannas says he's opposed to capital punishment, and Thibedeau replies, "People like you who oppose punishing criminals make me sick." (Johannas did not say he opposed punishing criminals.) When constructing an argument, remember to be fair and argue against what your opponents said, not your version of what they said.

There are many methods of trying to prove something. The types of reasoning explained above (cause and effect; comparisons; generalizations; proof by evidence, example, or authority; and debate) are all methods of proof to be considered when evaluating historical arguments. The next section examines assumptions, which are like reasoning in that they lead to conclusions (assertions). They are different from reasoning, however, in that they are not always consciously argued. Authors frequently do not realize the assumptions they are making.

## Assumptions

An assumption is the part of an argument containing the ideas or opinions that the arguer takes for granted. Stated assumptions are not of concern for the purposes of this Guide. When authors say they are assuming something, all you decide is whether you agree with the stated assumption.

Unstated assumptions are more difficult to recognize. There are two types of unstated assumptions: the general, more encompassing type and the specific type.

### GENERAL UNSTATED ASSUMPTIONS

These assumptions are part of the argument as a whole and, as such, cannot be identified by rewriting particular arguments. In any argument there are an infinite number of such assumptions. For example, if you say you are going to the store to buy a TV, you are making the general assumptions that the store will be there, that you won't die on the way, that they'll have televisions in stock, and so forth. Some assumptions are trivial or unlikely, but others are very important. For example, if the President of the United States says, "We will not agree to the Soviet proposal to have both countries eliminate half of their missiles because we cannot check on them adequately," he is assuming the Soviets cannot be trusted. If, on the other hand, the President agreed to missile reductions without a means of verifying Soviet reductions, he would then be assuming the Soviets can be trusted. He might or might not be right in either case. The important point is that we should recognize his assumption.

General assumptions shape historical interpretations. A historian who assumes that economics drives people's behavior will select economic information and write from that perspective; a historian who assumes that politics, in the form of power and compromise, shapes society will focus on that area in both research and writing.

### SPECIFIC UNSTATED ASSUMPTIONS

To understand specific unstated assumptions you need to know something about the form of arguments. As was explained in the section on **Assertions**, arguments are made up of the conclusion and the rest of the argument, which is designed to prove the conclusion. The sentences that comprise the rest of the argument are called *premises*.

Short arguments take the form of *premise, premise, conclusion*. A well-known example is: "Socrates is a man. All men are mortal. Therefore, Socrates is mortal." In premise, premise, conclusion format, this would be:

*Premise:*     Socrates is a man.

*Premise:*     All men are mortal.

*Conclusion:*     Therefore, Socrates is mortal.

If the above argument "looks funny," it's because people rarely talk this way. In normal speech, we often state the conclusion first: "I should be able to go outside now. My homework is done." It is also common to not state one of the premises or the conclusion at all. For example, if we are trying to decide who should pay for the broken vase, you might say, "Well, Joaquin pushed me into it." Your point (although you did not state it) is that Joaquin should pay.

When you leave out a premise, you are making an assumption. For example, the argument "We should spend our vacation in the mountains because we need a rest," can be rewritten this way:

*Premise:* We need a rest.

*Premise:* ??

*Conclusion:* (Therefore) we should spend our vacation in the mountains.

The missing premise is the assumption.

IDENTIFYING ASSUMPTIONS

You can figure out what the assumption is by asking, "What has to be true for this conclusion to be true?" In the above case, the missing premise (assumption) is: "The mountains are a good place to rest."

EVALUATING ASSUMPTIONS

When you have identified an assumption, evaluate it by asking if the assumption is correct. Assumptions are frequently related to the beliefs and values of the author, as explained in the next section.

## Values

Values are conditions that the person making an argument believes are important, worthwhile, or intrinsically good for themselves, their family, their country, and their world. Money, success, friendship, love, health, peace, power, freedom, and equality are examples of things people may value.

It is often important to discover the underlying values of the author of an argument, since assumptions made by an author are often related to the author's beliefs and values. This will help you understand why the viewpoint is argued the way it is, and, in cases where your values may be different from the author's values, it will help you understand why you might disagree with the argument. For example, if you believe that peace is more important than demonstrating power, then you are going to disagree with an argument which says that since Country A increased its power by attacking Country B; it was right to attack.

IDENTIFYING VALUE STATEMENTS

Clues to an author's value judgments are found in sentences containing words such as "good," "bad," "right," "wrong," "justified," "should," or "should not." For example, if someone says "The United States was wrong (value judgment) to drop the atomic bomb on Hiroshima because so many people were killed," that person is saying that life (value) is more important than the other conditions or values involved (power, peace vs. war, etc.).

To help identify an author's values, ask:
- Who wrote this?
- What beliefs does this person hold?

When you have identified a value judgment in an argument, you can then examine it. For example, consider the argument, "We should have capital punishment because criminals will commit fewer crimes if they think they might be executed."

EVALUATING VALUE
STATEMENTS

---

1. *Separate the argument into its factual and value parts.*
   Factual part:
   > Capital punishment will make criminals commit fewer crimes. (Notice that this could be investigated by examining statistics on the number of crimes with and without capital punishment.)

   Value assumption:
   > Fewer crimes is good (a desirable outcome).

2. *Rephrase the value statement into general terms.*
   > *Anything* (general term) which causes fewer crimes is good (value judgment).

3. *Ask yourself if the value statement is right in all instances.*
   > Is the statement, "Anything which causes fewer crimes is good" true? Can you think of cases in which you might not agree? Substitute some specific situations and see if the statement is still right. For example, "Jailing all people accused of a crime, whether found guilty or not, would also cause fewer crimes to be committed. Should we do this?"

---

This kind of questioning will help both you and the person who originally made the claim think more fully about the value(s) behind the claim.

Three general questions can be used to test the worthiness of value claims.
- Are you willing to use this value in all situations?
- What would society be like if everyone believed and acted on this value?
- Would you want the value applied to you?

The next page contains two charts you may find helpful for reminding you of methods you can use to analyze the viewpoints presented in this book. As you proceed, refer to this "Guide to Critical Thinking" to help you with the lessons.

# A MODEL FOR ANALYZING ARGUMENTS

A model is a way of organizing information. One type of model is an acronym where each letter in the model stands for a word. The model outlined here is **ARMEAR**. Each letter will remind you of a part of arguments to examine.

| | | |
|---|---|---|
| *A* | Author | • Who wrote this interpretation and why?<br>• What are the author's values or beliefs?<br>• What can you learn about the author? |
| *R* | Relevant Information | • What do you know about the topic being argued or topics related to it? |
| *M* | Main Point | • What is the main point or thesis of the argument? |
| *E* | Evidence | • What evidence is presented to support the argument?<br>• How reliable is it?<br>• What are the sources of the evidence? |
| *A* | Assumptions | • What assumptions does the author make? |
| *R* | Reasoning | • What reasoning is used in the argument? Cause and effect? Comparison? Generalization? Proof? Debate?<br>• How strong is the reasoning? |

# FIVE MAIN PARTS OF AN ARGUMENT

| | |
|---|---|
| **Assertion, main point, or thesis** | • What is the author trying to prove? |
| **Evidence** | • Is the source given for information?<br>• How strong is it? Primary? Reason to distort? Other evidence to verify? Public or private? (**PROP**). |
| **Reasoning** | • Cause and Effect — Is the connection shown? Are there other possible causes? Is there an important cause previous to the one proposed?<br>• Comparisons — How are the two cases different and how are they similar?<br>• Generalizations — How large and representative is the sample?<br>• Proof — Does the evidence support the point being made? How many examples are given? Is this authority an expert on this topic?<br>• Debate — Does the author attack other views in a fair way? Have all possible alternatives been eliminated? |
| **Assumptions** | • What must be true if the thesis is true (acceptable)? |
| **Values** | • Do I agree with these values?<br>• Is this value position right in all instances? |

# UNITED STATES AS A WORLD POWER

## LESSON 1      Identifying and Evaluating Sources

### Identifying Sources

One question we need to ask about any claim is whether a source is offered in support of it.

**Q** Label each item below with the appropriate letter.

    **S**    A **source** of information is given.

    **N**    **No** source of information is given.

_____1.    I think the movie "Roger Rabbit" is worth seeing. Both Megan and Pedro said they liked it.

_____2.    I checked their report cards, and ten of these students did not do well in chemistry last year. They have no business being in physics this year.

_____3.    The United States should not interfere in the internal affairs of other countries. Each country should settle its own problems.

_____4.    China was one of the weakest countries in the world in the late 1800s. Just look at her humiliating defeat in the Sino-Japanese War.

_____5.    Some Americans in the 1890s supported expansion for economic reasons. For example, Senator Albert Beveridge, in a speech delivered in Indianapolis, September 16, 1898, said we should expand into other countries to market our excess goods.

_____6.    In the late 1800s many Americans wanted a strong navy.

### Primary Sources

A primary source is evidence (often written) given by a person who was part of, or present at, the event reported. A primary source may also be an object that was part of the event.

> To determine the type of source, ask yourself:
> * Were the people doing the reporting part of the event?
> * Did they see the event on which they are reporting?
> If so, it is a primary source.

*[Continued on next page.]*

*[Continued from previous page.]*

**Q** Label each item below with the appropriate letter.

**P** The source is a **primary** source.

**S** The source is a **secondary** source.

_____7. Bob said he heard that the new 10th grade student is a good baseball player.

_____8. Rachel said the movie got a great review in the newspaper.

_____9. In his book *The New Empire* (Ithaca, New York: Cornell University Press, 1963) Walter La Feber said that America's expansion in the 1890s was partly due to the surplus goods produced by the Industrial Revolution.

_____10. President McKinley stated in a magazine interview in 1903 that, while he was praying for guidance from God, he decided the United States should keep control of the Philippines.

_____11. President Wilson, in an address to Congress on April 19, 1916, said that unless Germany stopped sinking passenger and freight ships immediately, the United States would be forced to break diplomatic relations with Germany.

_____12. Thomas Bailey, in *A Diplomatic History of the American People* (New York: Appleton, 1964), described British and German violations of American neutral rights in 1914 and 1915 and American reactions to those violations.

## Reason to Lie

People have a reason to lie if their statements help their own interests (for example, when they make more money) or make themselves or their group look good. People generally have no reason to lie if their statements make themselves look bad or their enemy look good.

> When questioning the truthfulness of a source, ask yourself:
> * Does the statement make the speaker (or group) look good?
> * Does the statement further or improve the interests of the speaker (or the group)?
> If so, then the source has a reason to lie.

*[Continued on next page.]*

*[Continued from previous page.]*

 Label each item below with the appropriate letter.

**R**  The person has a **reason** to lie.

**N**  The person has **no** reason to lie.

_____ 13.  Linda admitted she stole the gloves.

_____ 14.  Henry's pipe was found at the scene of the crime. (Does the pipe have a reason to lie?)

_____ 15.  William Jennings Bryan said in a speech that he opposed the United States taking over new lands, such as the Philippines, because the Bible emphasized love, not power and imperialism.

_____ 16.  Woodrow Wilson said in Congress on April 2, 1917, "It is a fearful thing to lead these great, peaceful people into war....But the right is more precious than peace, and we shall fight for the things which we have always carried nearest our hearts, for democracy..., for the rights and liberties of small nations...and [to] make the world itself at last free."

_____ 17.  On January 19, 1917, German Foreign Secretary Alfred Zimmermann sent a secret note to the German minister (diplomat) in Mexico. This note proposed a German-Mexican alliance against the United States if the United States did not remain neutral in World War I. It also told the minister to keep the proposal in the strictest secrecy.

_____ 18.  Historian Howard Beale has said that a large navy was an important part of expansionist policies in the late 1800s.

# LESSON 2    Evaluating Evidence

## Evaluate the Sources

 Evaluate the following pieces of evidence by listing strengths and weaknesses of each. If you need help, refer to the section on **Evidence** in the "Guide to Critical Thinking" (Unit 1).

1.  We are trying to determine if American leaders were interested in the Philippines (which was a Spanish colony) when the United States declared war on Spain in April 1898. We find a secret cable signed by Assistant Secretary of the Navy Theodore Roosevelt, dated just before war was declared. The cable tells Commodore Dewey, Roosevelt's friend, to be ready to attack the Spanish fleet in the Philippines in case war is declared.

    STRENGTHS:                      WEAKNESSES:

2.  In *The National Experience* (New York: Harcourt, Brace, Jovanovich, 1981), historian John Blum says that in 1902 President Theodore Roosevelt was anxious to build a canal through Panama (a region of Columbia). Blum says Roosevelt was angry when Columbia rejected the United States offer to buy the land, and let it be known that he would be in favor of a Panamanian revolution. According to Blum, Roosevelt helped the Panamanian revolutionists become independent of Columbia so the new country would allow the United States to build the canal.

    STRENGTHS:                      WEAKNESSES:

3.  We want to know if the United States entered World War I primarily to further its economic interests. We find a secret note dated September 6, 1915, sent by Secretary of State Robert Lansing to President Wilson. In the note, Lansing says that loaning Britain and France money would help America's balance of

*[Continued on next page.]*

*[Continued from previous page.]*

trade and the economy in general. (We already have evidence that the loans caused other problems which led to America's entry into the war.)

STRENGTHS:                    WEAKNESSES:

**Q** Choose the most reliable piece of evidence for each item, then explain your choice in the space provided.

4.  Which document would be most reliable in assessing why the United States entered World War I?

_____A.  Woodrow Wilson's message to Congress declaring war

_____B.  The 1930 memoirs of Colonel House (an advisor to Wilson) explaining Wilson's motives

_____C.  A memo from the State Department to President Wilson listing the pros and cons of declaring war

_____D.  A memo from Wilson to Colonel House explaining why he was going to declare war.

Explain your choice.

5.  Which document would be most reliable in assessing why Germany declared war on Russia in July 1914?

_____A.  The public war declaration by Kaiser Wilhelm (Germany's leader)

_____B.  The secretary's notes of a meeting between Wilhelm and his advisers to decide whether to declare war

_____C.  A German newspaper editorial from July 1914 on why Germany declared war

_____D.  A speech by Czar Nicholas of Russia on why Germany declared war on Russia

Explain your choice.

# LESSON 3        Determining Causes and Effects

Cause-and-effect reasoning argues that something caused, led to, or brought about something else.

 Label each item below with the appropriate letter.

> **C**    Item illustrates **cause-and-effect** reasoning.
>
> **N**    Item does **not** illustrate cause-and-effect reasoning.

For those items that you identify as cause and effect, write the cause and the effect in the space provided.

_____1.    Captain Alfred Thayer Mahan argued in 1890 that sea power made and kept nations great.

   CAUSE:                                EFFECT:

_____2.    In 1893 American settlers in Hawaii overthrew the Queen and put in a pro-American government. The settlers did this to make Hawaii part of the United States.

   CAUSE:                                EFFECT:

_____3.    Henry Cabot Lodge wanted a large navy and American expansion into Hawaii, Panama, the Caribbean Islands, and even Greenland.

   CAUSE:                                EFFECT:

_____4.    The 1898 war with Spain lasted only a few months but cost the United States $250 million.

   CAUSE:                                EFFECT:

*[Continued on next page.]*

*[Continued from previous page.]*

_____5.    The Platt Amendment became a permanent treaty between the United States and Cuba in 1903.

CAUSE:                          EFFECT:

_____6.    President Theodore Roosevelt's foreign affairs motto was, "speak softly and carry a big stick."

CAUSE:                          EFFECT:

**Q**  For each of the following situations, think of as many possible causes as you can, then evaluate the strength of the explanation given.

7.  Why are some people attractive? List at least four reasons.

"For that attractive look, try new Sunbaked Jeans."

a.    How strong do you think the above explanation is?

b.    Support your opinion.

8.  Why might a leader from one country negotiate a settlement between two other warring countries? List as many reasons you can.

*[Continued on next page.]*

*[Continued from previous page.]*

"President Theodore Roosevelt negotiated a settlement in the Russo-Japanese War in 1905 to prevent Japan from crushing Russia and thereby becoming more dominant in Asia."

    a.     How strong do you think the above explanation is?

    b.     Support your opinion.

9.  Why might the defenders, rather than the attackers, have the advantage in a war? List as many reasons as you can.

"In World War I the defense had the advantage due to the machine gun, which wiped out attackers in large numbers."

    a.     How strong do you think the above explanation is?

    b.     Support your opinion.

## LESSON 4          Assessing Cause-and-Effect Reasoning

### Identifying Cause-and-Effect Connections

The section on **Cause-and-Effect Reasoning** in the "Guide to Critical Thinking" (Unit 1) tells you that one question you should ask of any cause-and-effect argument is "Is there a connection between the cause and the effect?" This part of the lesson focuses on identifying that connection.

In April of 1898, the United States declared war on Spain. In the 1890s the Cubans had revolted against their colonial masters, the Spanish, who had used some harsh methods in their attempt to put down the rebellion. Although historians disagree as to how important it was, the Cuban situation was a factor in the American decision to go to war. Historians have advanced several theories as to the main cause of the United States declaration of war. One theory proposed that the "yellow press" (exaggerated and sensationalized stories in American newspapers) was the primary reason.

 Below are three historical arguments which all say that the yellow press was the main cause. Decide which of the three arguments is strongest and explain why. Pay particular attention to the connection between the proposed cause and the effect.

---

### Historian A

The main cause of the Spanish-American War was the yellow press. These penny newspapers competed for city readers so they could sell more advertising. This was especially true in New York City, where the papers owned by William Randolph Hearst and Joseph Pulitzer were in fierce competition. Each paper tried to outdo the other in printing the gruesome details of the Cuban revolution. As a result, the American public became sympathetic to the rebels, and the United States declared war to help the Cubans against the Spanish.

---

### Historian B

The main cause of the Spanish-American War was the yellow press. These newspapers, which competed for readers, often exaggerated and distorted the situation in Cuba. As William Randolph Hearst said to an artist in 1898, "You furnish the pictures; I'll furnish the war." Millions of Americans were influenced by the newspapers. With the 1898 elections approaching, both the Congress and President McKinley were quite aware of the public sentiment to protect the Cubans by declaring war with Spain.

---

*[Continued on next page.]*

*[Continued from previous page.]*

## Historian C

The main cause of the Spanish-American War was the yellow press. These newspapers exaggerated the situation in Cuba. For example, the *New York World* declared, "The horrors of the barbarous struggle [by the Spanish] for the extermination [destruction] of the native population [Cubans] are witnessed in all parts of the country." The papers also printed graphic drawings of the Cuban revolution. With such distortions in the papers, the country could not help but be pushed into war.

1. Which of the three arguments is strongest? Why do you think so? (Remember, this question is essentially asking "Which argument makes the strongest connection between the cause and the effect?")

## Evaluating Cause-and-Effect Arguments

 Fill in the diagram for each cause-and-effect argument below, then use the information in the diagram to evaluate the strength of the argument.

2. The woman's rent was raised by $50 per month, so she had to get a second, part-time job.

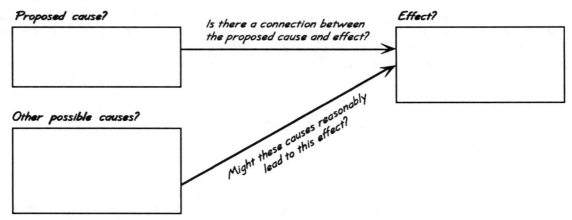

Proposed cause?

Is there a connection between the proposed cause and effect?

Effect?

Other possible causes?

Might these causes reasonably lead to this effect?

How strong is this argument? Why do you think so?

*[Continued on next page.]*

*[Continued from previous page.]*

3. The United States wanted to build a canal in Central America to help the American Navy and to improve trade. Columbia would not agree to sell the land needed to build the canal at the price the United States offered. This led to America's support for the Panamanian revolution against Columbia (Panama was a region in Columbia at the time), in hopes that the new country (Panama) would allow the United States to build the canal.

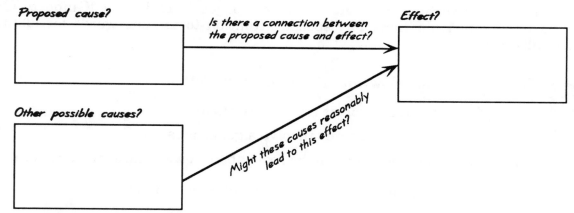

How strong is this argument? Why do you think so?

4. Many Chinese resented the way they were treated by foreigners in China in the late 1800s. These Chinese joined the Boxers, a secret anti-foreigner society, and staged a rebellion in 1900 to throw out the "foreign devils."

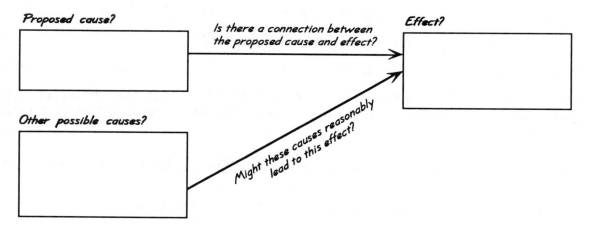

How strong is this argument? Why do you think so?

# LESSON 5     Analyzing Generalizations

## Identifying Generalizations

Refer to the section on **Generalization** pages 8–11 in the "Guide to Critical Thinking" (Unit 1) for help. Pay special attention to the cue words for identifying generalizations.

 Label each item below with the appropriate letter.

      **G**   The item involves a **generalization**.

      **N**   The item does **not** involve a generalization.

_____1.   Yushi took her car in to be fixed about a week after the accident.

_____2.   We do not have any male cheerleaders at our school.

_____3.   Everyone in our family is left-handed.

_____4.   Most Americans supported United States entry into World War I.

_____5.   President McKinley decided in April 1898 to ask for a declaration of war against Spain.

## Evaluating Generalizations

> The key question for evaluating generalizations is:
>
> • How large and representative is the sample?

 The sample taken should have the same subgroups in the same proportions as the whole population. Use these considerations to evaluate each generalization below.

6.  Team members have to dress up on game days. Otherwise, boys rarely, if ever, wear a dress shirt and tie to school.

How strong is this generalization? Why do you think so?

*[Continued on next page.]*

*[Continued from previous page.]*

7.  A June 1989 telephone survey of 1005 randomly selected adults showed that 54% could name the judge on the "People's Court" television show, while only 9% could name the Chief Justice of the Supreme Court. Most Americans know more about television judges than about the real Supreme Court judges.

    How strong is this generalization? Why do you think so?

8.  Many Americans were saddened and angered that the United States was involved in fighting over—and taking land in—other areas of the world during 1898 and the following years. They were especially upset that the United States was fighting the Filipinos.

    How strong is this generalization? Why do you think so?

9.  In the 1916 election Woodrow Wilson campaigned on the platform that he had kept the United States out of war while protecting America's neutral rights. Wilson received about 9,129,000 of the popular votes to 8,538,000 for the Republican candidate, Charles Evans Hughes. Wilson also won the electoral college, 277 to 254, when he carried California by a mere 4000 votes.

    How strong is this generalization? Why do you think so?

# LESSON 6    Why Did President McKinley Ask for a Declaration of War against Spain in April 1898?

On April 11, 1898, President McKinley addressed Congress to ask for a declaration of war against Spain. This lesson presents two viewpoints of why he did this.

## Historian A

(1) The Spanish-American War was a key event in American imperialism. As such, it is important to understand how the United States became involved in the war. It is clear from the records left to us that President McKinley was pushed into the war by jingoists (militaristic patriots who frequently want war) and the press. The President did not really want war, but he was too weak-willed to stand up against the popular demand for military action.

(2) When McKinley entered the presidency in March 1897, he was surrounded by a group of expansionists, including Senator Henry Cabot Lodge, Assistant Secretary of the Navy Theodore Roosevelt, and Captain Alfred T. Mahan. These men wanted a large navy, a string of naval bases, and territorial and trade expansion.[1] When the situation in Cuba worsened, President McKinley had already been advised to pursue expansionist policies.

(3) Meanwhile, the Spanish were having great difficulty ruling Cuba in the 1890s. The United States had passed the Wilson-Gorman Tariff in 1894, which put a 40-percent duty (tax) on sugar from Cuba. The sugar plantations were ruined, and since Cuba's economy depended almost completely on sugar, the whole economy fell apart. The Cuban people suffered greatly, and a rebellion against the Spanish soon resulted.[2] The Spanish, under General Weyler, were forced to use harsh measures, such as herding Cuban people into *reconcentrados* (concentration camps), to suppress the revolt.

(4) As bad as the Spanish actions were, they were not sufficient to cause the United States to declare war—countries frequently use violence and cruelty to crush revolutions, but other governments do not declare war on them. Besides, many Americans realized that the rebels were just as harsh as the Spanish.

(5) The yellow press escalated (increased) the Cuban situation into a declaration of war. The newspapers in New York City competed for readers, because the more readers a paper had, the more it could charge for advertising. Readers could be gained through sensational stories, and many such stories could be written about the rebellion in Cuba. Day after day, Americans read about General Weyler's atrocities (tortures, killing of civilians, war crimes) toward Cuban men, women, and children.[3] Graphic drawings were also included. Much of what was written was exaggerated or distorted—the yellow press was more interested in selling papers than in printing the truth. As William Randolph Hearst told an artist in 1898, "You furnish the pictures; I'll furnish the war."[4]

(6) American public opinion against Spain was inflamed in February 1898

*[Continued on next page.]*

## Historian A

*[Continued from previous page.]*

by two events. First, a letter by the Spanish minister, de Lôme, was published in a New York newspaper. In it, de Lôme referred to McKinley as a weak man who was a "bidder for the admiration of the crowd."[5] Second, the American battleship *Maine* was blown up in Havana (Cuba) Harbor, killing 260 Americans. Americans immediately believed that the Spanish had torpedoed the ship. The American press had a field day with these two events, whipping up public outrage to new heights.[6]

(7) Faced with this public pressure, McKinley sent Spain a series of harsh demands on March 27, 1898. Except for a few minor points, the Spanish agreed to the demands.[7] By this time, however, McKinley was being pressed by the jingoists to declare war. Moreover, McKinley did not want Congress to take the initiative in declaring war, since it would look like he, the President, was a weak leader. If McKinley looked weak, his Republican Party would be hurt in the upcoming fall Congressional elections.[8]

(8) So McKinley ignored the Spanish concessions and went before Congress on April 11, 1898, to lead the country into war. In reality, McKinley did not lead the country at all; he allowed himself to be pushed into an imperialistic war by public opinion and an elite group of militaristic patriots. As Senator Spooner said, "The President could have avoided war, but the press and jingoists were too strong and the fall elections were too near."

## *Endnotes for Historian A*

[1] Henry Cabot Lodge, "Our Blundering Foreign Policy," *The Forum*, Vol. XIX (March 1895), pp. 14–17:

> "In the interests of our commerce and of our fullest development we should build the Nicaragua Canal...control the Hawaiian Islands and maintain our influence in Samoa....When the Nicaragua Canal is built, the island of Cuba...will become to us a necessity."

Alfred T. Mahan, "The United States Looking Outward," *The Atlantic Monthly*, Vol. LXVI (1890), pp. 821–23:

> "Whether they will or not, Americans must now begin to look outward. The growing production of the country demands it. An increasing volume of public sentiment [feelings] demands it."

[2] Thomas A. Bailey, *A Diplomatic History of the American People*, eighth edition (New York, 1969), p. 451:

> "The American tariff of 1894, by placing relatively high duties on sugar, visited the island with economic prostration [reduced to helplessness]. Early in 1895, the unhappy Cubans unfurled the flag of rebellion."

[3] *New York Journal*, February 23, 1896, 27: 1, 2, 3:

> "It is not only Weyler the soldier—but Weyler the brute, the devastator of haciendas [homes], the destroyer of families, and the outrager of women—pitiless, cold, an exterminator of men...."

*New York World*, May 17, 1896, 1:8, 2:1:

> "Blood on the roadsides, blood in the fields, blood on the doorsteps, blood, blood, blood! The old, the young, the weak, the crippled—all are butchered without mercy."

[4] There is a story that Hearst said this to the artist Frederick Remington. J. R. Winkler, *W. R. Hearst* (New York, 1928), p. 144.

[5] J. B. Moore, *A Digest of International Law* (Washington, 1906), VI, 176.

[6] For example, Hearst's newspaper printed the headlines:

*[Continued on next page.]*

## *Endnotes for Historian A*

*[Continued from previous page.]*

"THE WARSHIP MAINE WAS SPLIT IN TWO BY ENEMY'S SECRET INFERNAL MACHINE"

"THE WHOLE COUNTRY THRILLS WITH WAR FEVER"

[7] McKinley's demands on March 27, 1898, were (summarized by the author of this book):

First: Armistice (truce) until October 1.

Second: Immediate ending of *reconcentrado* policy.

Third: The President of the United States to be the final arbiter (judge) between Spain and the Cuban rebels, if terms of peace are not settled between Spain and the Cubans by October 1.

Within the next two weeks Spain announced an armistice and an end to the *reconcentrado* policy. This was all Spain could be expected to do, under the circumstances.

[8] Letter from Senator Henry Cabot Lodge to President McKinley:

"[I]f the war in Cuba drags on through the summer with nothing done we shall go down in the greatest defeat [in the fall elections] ever known."

---

## Historian B

(1) The causes of the Spanish-American War have been studied by historians for years. While a number of interpretations have been advanced, the common view is that President McKinley was a weak leader who was pushed into war by a small number of jingoists and the yellow press. Close examination of the causes of the war, however, shows that the common view is mistaken. President McKinley was actually a strong leader who knew what he wanted—he did not need public opinion to push him into war.

(2) The theory that a group of influential jingoists was a key factor in the war is wrong. Assistant Secretary of the Navy Theodore Roosevelt, Senator Henry Cabot Lodge and other jingoists actually had little influence with McKinley—much less than Assistant Secretary of State William R. Day, Senator William B. Allison, and several other men (none of whom were jingoists).[1] How then could the jingoists have talked McKinley into war?

(3) Likewise, the theory of yellow journalism does not explain the war. The president can ignore public opinion if he chooses. It must be remembered that newspapers could not create public opinion on the war issue but only shape pre-existing opinion. Historians have mistakenly taken seriously William Randolph Hearst's statement that he would furnish the war. Hearst exaggerated his own role in what he considered to be a "splendid little war."

(4) President McKinley's clear-cut goals show that he, not the jingoists or yellow press, was in control of United States policy. The president was worried about German expansion, but could do little about it while American interests and energies were focused on Cuba.[2] Thus, McKinley wanted the difficulties between Spain and her colony resolved. As long as the hostilities in Cuba continued, the United States looked weak.

(5) McKinley tried to resolve the conflict in Cuba without war by submitting a proposal to Spain calling for Cuban autonomy (self-government). The de Lôme letter undermined his efforts for a peaceful solution, but not because de Lôme said the President was weak. Rather, the letter showed that Spanish promises of reform in Cuba were

*[Continued on next page.]*

## Historian B

*[Continued from previous page.]*

not being carried out—Spain was telling the United States one thing but doing another.[3]

(6) When the battleship *Maine* was blown up, the American public clamored for war. President McKinley set up a naval board of inquiry to study the incident—he was not being herded into war. If the destruction of the *Maine* was the reason for war, why was it two months before the United States acted?

(7) In late March McKinley sent a series of stiff demands to Spain. Spain's response to the demands has been misinterpreted by historians. While Spain seemed to concede to most of the demands, in reality she did not. Most importantly, Spain would not agree to independence for Cuba.[4] This was the central point in McKinley's program.

(8) In light of evidence (the de Lôme letter) showing that the Spanish had negotiated in bad faith, and in light of the lack of agreement on McKinley's main demand, war could scarcely be avoided. What led to the Spanish-American War was not the jingoists and yellow press, but rather, President McKinley's conscious policy[5] of independence for Cuba. To this the Spanish could not, and would not, agree.

### *Endnotes for Historian B*

[1] Horace Samuel and Marion Galbraith Merrill, *The Republican Command, 1897–1913*, (The University Press of Kentucky, 1971), p. 1:

"At the beginning of 1897, President William McKinley and a coterie [small group] of senators, called 'The Four,' constituted the top command [of the Republican Party]. The four were Nelson W. Aldrich of Rhode Island, Orville H. Platt of Connecticut, William B. Allison of Iowa, and John C. Spooner of Wisconsin. [Later Theodore Roosevelt, Joseph G. Cannon, and William Howard Taft joined the group.]

"No other Republicans wielded the great power over policy, legislation, nominations, and appointments that these eight [including McKinley] possessed."

[2] Germany sent warships into Haiti in the winter of 1897, defied the Monroe Doctrine, and announced plans to build new warships for the Caribbean and South Atlantic. Germany also took over part of China in November 1897, but the United States could do nothing about it as long as Cuba occupied so much of its attention.

[3] There was evidence in de Lôme's letter showing that neither Spain's announced reforms in Cuba, nor Spain's negotiations for a trade pact with the United States were being carried out sincerely.

"Without a military end of the matter nothing will be accomplished in Cuba. [This indicates that he felt Spain should defeat the Cuban rebels rather than reform the island.]

"It would be very advantageous to take up *even if only for effect*, the question of commercial relations [with the United States]." Emphasis added. (This shows that he wanted Spain to discuss commercial relations merely to improve Spain's image in the United States.)

Letter from Enrique Depuy de Lôme to Don Jose Canaljas (a friend of de Lôme), December 1897, from *Foreign Relations of the United States* (1898), p. 1007.

[4] McKinley's demands were that Spain:

First: Declare an immediate armistice (truce) lasting until October 1.

Second: Permanently abolish the *reconcentrado* policy.

Third: Permit the President to mediate (help the Spanish and Cubans come to an agreement) if a settlement between Spain and the rebels was not reached during the armistice.

The third demand involved Cuban independence, since McKinley, as mediator, could require it. Both

*[Continued on next page.]*

## Endnotes for Historian B
*[Continued from previous page.]*

the Spanish and the Americans realized that the third demand was the most important.

Spain agreed to the first two demands, but McKinley wondered about Spain's sincerity. Then Assistant Secretary of State Day asked the Spanish whether they were ready to grant Cuban independence. The answer was no. So actually, the Spanish reply to the United States demands was completely unsatisfactory.

[5] One event which shows that the President, not the jingoists or yellow press, was in control of events was a speech on Cuba given by Senator Redfield Proctor. The republican from Vermont, who had just returned from a tour of Cuba, inflamed the American public with his speech describing the terrible cruelties practiced by the Spanish and calling for Cuban independence.

Stories at the time make it seem likely that McKinley had sent Senator Proctor to Cuba and approved his speech before its delivery. The President was as much in control of public opinion as was the yellow press.

 ## Historian A

1. The main point of Historian A is:

_____A. The Spanish gave in to American demands, so President McKinley should not have asked for a declaration of war.

_____B. The Spanish-American War was a key event in American history.

_____C. President McKinley was pushed into war by the *jingoists* and the yellow press.

_____D. The destruction of the *Maine* forced President McKinley to ask for a declaration of war.

2. What is the unstated assumption in the second paragraph? (See **Assumptions** in the "Guide to Critical Thinking" (Unit 1) pp. 15–16 for the steps for identifying unstated assumptions.)

3. Determine the type of reasoning (cause and effect, comparison, generalization, or proof) and key question for each of the following sections taken from Historian A, then decide how well the argument answers the key question. Boxes have been provided for your answers and the first one has been done for you.

a. "The United States had passed the Wilson-Gorman Tariff in 1894, which put a 40-percent duty (tax) on sugar from Cuba. The sugar plantations were ruined, and since Cuba's economy depended almost completely on sugar, the

*[Continued on next page.]*

*[Continued from previous page.]*

whole economy fell apart. The Cuban people suffered greatly, and a rebellion against the Spanish soon resulted." (Paragraph 3)

| Type of Reasoning | Key Question | How Well Answered |
|---|---|---|
| Cause and Effect | Is there a good connection between the cause and the effect? (p. 5) | The author does show a connection by explaining that Cuba was dependent upon sugar exports. |

b. "The yellow press escalated (increased) the Cuban situation into a declaration of war." (Paragraph 5)

| Type of Reasoning | Key Question | How Well Answered |
|---|---|---|
| | | |

c. "Day after day, Americans read about General Weyler's atrocities (tortures, killing of civilians, war crimes) toward Cuban men, women, and children." (Paragraph 5)

| Type of Reasoning | Key Question | How Well Answered |
|---|---|---|
| | | |

d. "If McKinley looked weak, his Republican Party would be hurt in the upcoming fall Congressional elections." (Paragraph 7)

| Type of Reasoning | Key Question | How Well Answered |
|---|---|---|
| | | |

*[Continued on next page.]*

*[Continued from previous page.]*

    e.  "The Spanish, under General Weyler, were forced to use harsh measures, such as herding Cuban people into *reconcentrados* (concentration camps), to suppress the revolt. As bad as the Spanish actions were, they were not sufficient to cause the United States to declare war—countries frequently use violence and cruelty to crush revolutions, but other governments do not declare war on them." (Paragraph 3)

| Type of Reasoning | Key Question | How Well Answered |
|---|---|---|
|  |  |  |

4.    Evaluate the evidence put forth in:

  a.  Paragraph 5, last sentence

  b.  Paragraph 6, sentence 3

## [Q] Historian B

5.    The main point of Historian B is:

6.    What is the unstated assumption in the last sentence in paragraph 4?

*[Continued on next page.]*

*[Continued from previous page.]*

7.  Determine the type of reasoning (cause and effect, comparison, generalization, or proof) used in the following.

   a.  "The theory that a group of influential jingoists was a key factor in the war is wrong. Assistant Secretary of the Navy Theodore Roosevelt, Senator Henry Cabot Lodge and other jingoists actually had little influence with McKinley—much less than Assistant Secretary of State William R. Day, Senator William B. Allison and several other men (none of whom were jingoists). How then could the jingoists have talked McKinley into war?"

| Type of Reasoning | Key Question | How Well Answered |
|---|---|---|
|  |  |  |

   b.  "The president was worried about German expansion, but could do little about it while American interests and energies were focused on Cuba."

| Type of Reasoning | Key Question | How Well Answered |
|---|---|---|
|  |  |  |

   c.  "If the destruction of the *Maine* was the reason for war, why was it two months before the United States acted?"

| Type of Reasoning | Key Question | How Well Answered |
|---|---|---|
|  |  |  |

*[Continued on next page.]*

*[Continued from previous page.]*

 **General Questions**

8.  Given the relevant information in the box below, compare the evidence in endnote 4 (paragraph 7) for Historian B with endnote 7 (paragraph 7) for Historian A. Which viewpoint is stronger regarding Spain's reply to United States demands?

> Relevant Information
>
> A mediator is someone who brings the two sides in a dispute together to help them discuss their differences, but does not decide on a solution to the dispute.

# LESSON 7    Why Was the United States Imperialistic from 1890 to 1929?

## Background Information

This lesson presents two viewpoints of why the United States was imperialistic from 1890 to 1929. Imperialism means political control or economic domination of one country by another country.

The two viewpoints argue about trade (buying and selling goods with other countries), but more importantly about investments (people from Country A buying shares of businesses in Country B, or setting up whole businesses in Country B). Investments can sometimes lead to economic domination or economic imperialism.

One of the viewpoints is from the Marxist perspective that capitalism (private ownership of business) is doomed to failure. Marxists believe that as capital-

ists (business owners) compete for larger profits, prices decline due to overproduction (consumers cannot buy all the goods produced), and many businesses go bankrupt. This leads to monopolies (control of an industry by only one company) and exploitation (cheating) of the workers. Fewer and fewer people have more and more of the wealth. Eventually, the workers will overthrow the capitalist system and replace it with communism.

The central questions that the two viewpoints focus on are: Did the United States become interested in foreign countries because of desperate businessmen trying to find places to sell their excess products at higher prices? Or were other reasons more important?

## Historian A

(1) The United States was an imperialist country from 1890 to 1929. During this time the United States took over, or economically dominated, the Philippines, Cuba, Panama, Guam, Hawaii, Midway, Columbia, China, and others. United States foreign investments increased tremendously from $15 million in 1865 to $685 million in 1897 to $20 billion in 1929! The new American imperialism was more subtle than that of previous imperialist powers. Although the United States generally did not run the country politically (except in the Philippines), its economic investments controlled what the country did.

(2) The United States became imperialistic due to declining profits for

American businesses. As a capitalist country, the United States was moving toward widespread monopolies in the 1890s. More goods were being produced than Americans could consume. This led to declining prices (prices had to be cut in order to sell the excess goods) and thus to declining profits.[1] Influential businessmen within the United States, such as Charles Conant, recognized this trend. Conant stated in 1898, "New markets and new opportunities for investment must be found if surplus capital is to be profitably employed."[2] Not only did United States companies need to sell their excess goods, but they also had to invest their excess capital (money) outside the

*[Continued on next page.]*

## Historian A

*[Continued from previous page.]*

United States where it would lead to bigger profits and whole new markets—only in this way could economic stagnation and revolution by the poor in America be prevented.[3]

(3) There is no question that the United States was pushed into its imperialist adventures by monopolistic businessmen trying to save their profits from the decline of capitalism within the United States. For example, as a monopoly, the American Sugar Refining Company had received excessive profits in the United States. As its profits fell due to competition from within the United States, the company sought new markets in foreign countries. It benefited greatly from its investments in Cuba after the Spanish-American War, as well as from investments in other Central American states.

(4) It was businessmen who pushed the United States into taking the Philippines. Business groups argued to President McKinley that the Philippines should be held by the United States "for the protection and further-ance of the commercial interests of our citizens in the Far East"[4]—even though the Filipinos wanted independence. They also argued that with millions of Chinese within easy distance, we could greatly increase our trade by keeping the Philippines.[5]

(5) The net result upon the countries in which the United States invested was devastating. Precious resources, which the countries needed to help pull themselves out of poverty, were drained off to the United States. American companies, not the poor countries, made all the profits. Moreover, the poor workers were wage slaves to the giant companies, which exploited the workers with low wages while raking in enormous profits.

(6) Thus, from 1890 to 1929, the United States began its imperialist investments to save the monopolistic businessmen from the declining profits and collapse of capitalism which is inevitable in the capitalist system. In the process, underdeveloped (poor) countries were exploited and their growth retarded for decades.

## Endnotes for Historian A

[1] V. I. Lenin, *Imperialism: The Highest Stage of Capitalism.* Lenin was the leader of the 1917 Bolshevik (Communist) Revolution in Russia. Lenin argues that competitive capitalism leads to monopoly capitalism, which leads to overproduction and declining profits. This leads to imperialism in order to find new areas for profitable investment, and eventually to war as capitalist countries fight each other for these needed markets.

[2] Charles Conant, "The Economic Basis of Imperialism," *North American Review*, September 1898. He further stated, "The United States cannot afford to adhere to a policy of isolation while other nations are reaching out for the command of these new markets."

[3] Claude Julien, *America's Empire,* (New York: Vintage Books, 1971), p. 57:

"The economic crisis of 1893–1898 had incited many disorders [in the United States], with riots, hunger marches, explosions of violence which, for some people, foreshadowed a revolution."

Charles and Mary Beard, *A Basic History of the United States* (New York: Doubleday, Doran and Co., 1945), p. 339:

"A diversion of the people's thought from domestic discontent over plutocracy and poverty, such as embroiled the land in the campaign of 1896, to world politics and wars would damp if not extinguish radicalism at home."

*[Continued on next page.]*

## Endnotes for Historian A

*[Continued from previous page.]*

[4] *Journal of the American Asiatic Association*, I (1898), 1, quoted in Thomas J. McCormick, "Insular Imperialism and the Open Door: The Spanish-American War," *Pacific Historical Review* 32: 155–69, May 1963.

[5] Speech by Senator Henry Cabot Lodge, 1900, quoted in Leon Wolff, *Little Brown Brothers* (New York: Doubleday & Company, Inc., 1960), p. 304:

> "I believe to abandon the islands...would be a wrong to humanity...Manila, with its magnificent bay, is the prize and the pearl of the East...it will keep open to us the markets of China."

Albert J. Beveridge, speech in the Senate, January 8, 1900, summarized by Wolff:

> "Trade with China...was paramount to America's future, while the Philippines themselves abounded in rice, coffee, sugar, hemp, tobacco, copper and gold."

Mark Hanna, campaign speech for William McKinley (Republican) in 1900, quoted in Wolff:

> "If it is commercialism to want...a foothold [the Philippines] in the markets of that great Eastern country [China], for God's sake, let us have commercialism."

*Insurance Advocate* (business journal):

> "Keeping the Philippines would encourage 'the teeming millions of the Middle Kingdom [China] to buy from us.'"

---

## Historian B

(1) Some Marxist economists (such as V. I. Lenin) have argued that United States imperialism from 1890 to 1929 was due to businessmen's efforts to invest overseas because of declining profits on capital in the United States. They say that foreign investment was critical in propping up the profit rate for United States companies. This argument is erroneous, however, for several reasons.

(2) First, compared to total United States investments within the country, foreign investments were small. From 1869 to 1897, foreign investment was 1 percent of total investment. From 1900 to 1929, it was only 6 percent of total investment, making the increase in United States foreign investment smaller than the increase in California investment alone.

(3) Second, very few United States companies were involved significantly in foreign investment. Most companies did not invest abroad.[1] Except for agriculture, manufacturing, and metals, the amount put into foreign investment was less than .1 percent of total investment. Even for agriculture, manufacturing, and metals, the foreign investment was less than 2 percent of the total investment.

(4) Third, if it is true that foreign investment was critical in propping up sagging United States profit rates, then we should see a significant rise in profits from 1890 to 1929. But we do not see this; the United States profit rate went from about 4.8 percent in 1890 to about 4.9 percent in 1929.

(5) In only five industries—bananas, sugar, copper, oil, and precious metals (gold, silver, etc.)—was there significant foreign investment. Foreign investment in precious metals was around long before capitalism, so this investment cannot be said to be due to capitalist imperialism. There is no domestic supply of bananas, so foreign banana investment was understandable. Foreign oil investment, although

*[Continued on next page.]*

## Historian B

*[Continued from previous page.]*

significant, was still only 7 percent of total 1929 oil investment. This leaves only sugar and copper, in which high foreign investment might be due to declining profits within the United States.

(6) The picture of United States imperialism which emerges from this investigation is not surplus capital desperately searching for needed investment, but rather a few businessmen in a few industries seizing a chance to make more profits.

(7) The cases of Cuba and Panama illustrate the weaknesses of the Marxist argument. After the Spanish-American War and the Reciprocity Treaty of 1902, which lowered the United States tariff (import charge) on Cuban sugar, the American Sugar Refining Company seemed to have benefited. It was the landholders in Cuba, however, who really benefited. The amount of sugar refined by the American Sugar Refining Company did not increase significantly after 1902 because demand for sugar in the United States did not change significantly. Although from 1900 to 1903 Cuban sugar imports rose by 1.8 billion pounds, imports from the Dutch East Indies and Europe both fell by .9 billion pounds, offsetting it. The American Sugar Refining Company did not benefit from this increase in Cuban sugar exports because it did not own much land in Cuba. All Americans combined only owned 16 percent of the 1902 sugar crop. Thus, the monopolistic American Sugar Refining Company did not benefit significantly from the takeover of Cuba.

(8) In Panama, the United States received $110 million from 1909 to 1929 in Canal revenues, but had canal expenses of $816 million, for a loss of $706 million. One might argue that rich American stockholders in the Panama Canal Company reaped the profits from this loss to the taxpayers. Most of the stockholders, however, were French, not American. It might seem like American shippers made money by cutting shipping costs, but they received no advantage over competitors since shippers from every nation used the canal at the same cost. The reasonable viewpoint is that the United States built the canal, not for profits for businessmen, but for military reasons.

(9) Marxists also argue that workers were exploited in the countries Americans invested in. The evidence, however, shows that in this time period American companies paid wages equal to, and often higher than, the prevailing wage in these countries.[2] The workers were better off as a result of United States investments.

(10) Thus, American imperialism was not a result of pressure applied by American businessmen. The evidence does not support the theory that there was a push by businessmen to increase foreign investment, exploit impoverished foreign workers, and save themselves from the decline of monopoly capitalism.

*[Continued on next page.]*

*[Continued from previous page.]*

### Endnotes for Historian B

[1] Cleona Lewis, *America's Stake in International Investment* (1938).

[2] In Cuba, immigration of laborers was restricted, while exports of sugar tripled. Thus, demand for workers, and their wages, must have gone up. The average 1900–1901 wage for sugar workers was $.76 a day, but in January 1902, it was $.85$\frac{1}{2}$ a day.

In Columbia, the United Fruit Company (an American company) paid wages above the going wage. It paid wages in scrip, redeemable at the company store. But prices at the store were lower than in local stores, so workers' real wages were even higher. Frederick Rippy, *The Capitalists and Columbia*, pp. 190–91.

"Wages paid by United Fruit were high in comparison to money wages paid to agricultural workers elsewhere in Central America." Charles Kepner, Jr., *Social Aspects of the Banana Industry* (1936), p. 129."

 **Historian A**

1.  What is the main idea of Historian A?

2.  Evaluate the evidence in the following.

a.  Endnote 2

b.  Endnote 3

*[Continued on next page.]*

*[Continued from previous page.]*

3. Evaluate the argument in the following.

  a. Paragraph 4

  b. Paragraph 5

 **Historian B**

4. What is the main idea of Historian B?

5. Evaluate the evidence in the following.

  a. Endnote 1

*[Continued on next page.]*

*[Continued from previous page.]*
   b.  Endnote 2

6.   Evaluate the reasoning in the following.
  a.  Paragraph 2

   b.  Paragraph 4

   c.  Paragraph 8

7.   Overall, which viewpoint is stronger? Explain your answer.

## LESSON 8     Who Was Primarily to Blame for the *Lusitania* Tragedy?

## Background Information

From 1914 to 1917, the United States remained neutral while trying to decide whether to enter World War I on the British-French side against the Germans. One of the most spectacular events that occurred during this time of neutrality was the May 7, 1915, sinking of the British passenger liner, *Lusitania,* by a German submarine. This lesson presents two viewpoints of who was to blame for the tragedy. Dates in parentheses in the titles are the publication dates of the original interpretation.

### Historian A (1972)

*(1)* On May 7, 1915, a German U-boat (submarine) sank the British passenger liner, *Lusitania,* with the loss of some 1200 people. Most people have blamed the tragedy completely on the Germans. This view is wrong—the British were much more at fault than people ever believed.

*(2)* First, Germany published warnings in American newspapers that British passenger ships sailing into the submarine area around Great Britain would be sunk. Some nervous passengers on the *Lusitania* asked the captain about the warnings, and the captain reassured them that the *Lusitania* would be protected by British warships. Despite the reassurance, however, there was no protection by the British navy. The cruiser *Juno* was supposed to meet the *Lusitania* off the coast of Ireland and escort her to port, but the *Juno* was recalled to port and never met the passenger liner.[1] The British Admiralty knew there were submarines in the area and did not want a warship sunk. The *Lusitania* sailed unwarned and without benefit of an escort into an area where submarines were known to be active. [2]

*(3)* Second, the British navy did not tell the passengers that the ship was loaded with munitions and was outfitted to have guns mounted on her.[3] The British had decided to use passenger ships to protect shipments of badly-needed war materials and, to protect them further, they mounted guns on the ships (called mystery ships). The Germans were caught in a dilemma. If they left the ships alone, the English would get more materials with which to fight Germany. If the submarines surfaced to warn the ships, the "passenger" ships could sink the submarines with one hit (the submarines could not tell through a periscope if the ships were armed or not). If the submarines sank the passenger ships without warning, the British would cry "barbarity" and draw the United States into the war against Germany.

*(4)* The commander of the U–20 (the submarine which sank the *Lusitania*) had little choice but to attack the huge liner without warning. One torpedo—not two, as has been alleged for many years—hit the forward part of the ship.[4] This was followed by a second explo-

*[Continued on next page.]*

## Historian A

*[Continued from previous page.]*

sion, either from the tons of ammunition blowing up or the explosion of gun cotton. The gun cotton on the ship was for use in naval mines. It has the unusual characteristic of exploding when it comes into contact with ocean water![5] It was this second explosion which ripped out a large portion of the bottom of the ship and caused it to sink in only 18 minutes.

(5) Third, the *Lusitania's* poor design was a major factor in the great loss of life. Unlike the *Titanic*, which had transverse watertight compartments, the *Lusitania* had longitudinal compartments (see diagram A below).

(6) When the *Titanic* hit the iceberg, it took two hours to sink and did not list (lean to the side) because its compartments flooded all the way across the ship. Thus, all its lifeboats could be lowered. When the *Lusitania* was hit by the torpedo, the compartments on the opposite side of the ship did not flood right away. The ship went into a fifteen degree list within seconds; the list got much worse later (see diagram B, next page).

(7) This list prevented the lowering of most of the lifeboats. As shown in diagram B, the five-ton lifeboats on the high side of the *Lusitania* either swung in over the deck of the ship, slid down it and crushed passengers in their paths,[6] or slid down the side of the ship and were ripped open by the one-inch rivets sticking out from the side. The boats on the low side were difficult and dangerous to climb into and almost impossible to lower.

(8) Fourth, the British Admiralty recalled a ship (the *Juno* again) which could have rescued many of the passengers. The *Juno* was recalled within sight of the passengers because the British were afraid it, too, would be sunk by the submarine. It was more than two hours before other, smaller boats arrived. Darkness soon followed, and by the next morning most of the passengers had drowned.

(9) The British Admiralty conducted an inquiry into the sinking and blamed the whole matter on the Germans and the captain of the *Lusitania*, absolving itself of any responsibility. The Germans were guilty of barbarity, they concluded, and the captain of the liner did not heed Admiralty warnings of submarine activity and try to avoid the U-boat. There was no mention of munitions on the ship, the ship's design, or any other problems. The British government had what it wanted. The Germans looked like uncivilized brutes and the United States was very angry—well on its way to siding with Britain in the war.

## Diagram A

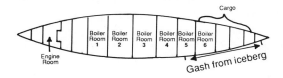

*Titanic* (Transverse compartments)

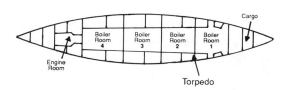

*Lusitania* (Longitudinal compartments)

*[Continued on next page.]*

*[Continued from previous page.]*

## Diagram B

Regular

With list

### *Endnotes for Historian A*

[1] Shortly after noon on May 5, the Admiralty signaled the *Juno* to abandon her escort mission and return to Queenstown. The *Lusitania* was not informed that she was now alone.

[2] Commander Kenworthy, who had previously submitted a paper at Sir Winston Churchill's request (Churchill was First Lord of the British Admiralty) on the political results of an ocean liner being sunk with American passengers on board, was called to a meeting in the Admiralty map room on May 5, 1915. What was said will never be known, but Kenworthy left the room disgusted at the cynical attitude of his superiors. He wrote later, "The *Lusitania* was sent at considerably reduced speed into an area where a U-boat was known to be waiting and with her escort withdrawn." He concluded that the Admiralty was letting the *Lusitania* be sunk to pull the United States into the war.

[3] The previous captain of the *Lusitania*, Captain Dow, protested the mixing of passengers and munitions. He was replaced by Captain Turner.

The records of the Remington Small Arms Company show that 2,000 cases of small arms ammunition were received by the *Lusitania*.

The *Lusitania* and her sister ship, the *Mauritania*, were built by the Cunard Company with the help of the British Admiralty. In time of war, the ships could be outfitted by the Admiralty as war ships. Extra plating and gun mounts were added to the *Lusitania*, but the guns were probably never put on.

[4] Diary of Captain Schwieger, Commander of the U–20, the submarine which torpedoed the *Lusitania*, May 7, 1915, 3:10 p.m.:

"Torpedo hits starboard side right behind the bridge. An unusually heavy detonation takes place with a very strong explosion cloud. The explosion of the torpedo must have been followed by a second one (boiler or coal or powder)."

[5] Dr. Ritter von Rettegh made a sworn statement of a conversation he had in Washington with Captain Guy Gaunt of the British navy:

"After some little conversation, he [Gaunt] asked me what effect, if any, sea water coming in contact with gun cotton would have. I inquired of him why he wanted to know this. He said, 'We are required to send by one of our fastest steamers [the *Lusitania* had set the record for the fastest crossing of the Atlantic] in the next day or so about six hundred tons of gun cotton, which we have purchased from Du Pont Powder Company.' I told him that if sea water comes into contact with the gun cotton immediately a chemical change takes place—raising the temperature and causing a sudden explosion. He asked me what to do to prevent this, and I said to keep it in a dry place."

It was not the boilers which exploded. The testimony of the two survivors of number 1 boiler room shows the boilers did not explode. They stated that they tried to escape for several minutes (the second explosion occurred right after the torpedo struck the ship), but did not mention any boilers blowing up. The survivor of number 2 boiler room also testified that the boilers did not explode. Number 3 and number 4 boiler rooms rose out of the water and were not close to the point where the torpedo struck the ship, so those boilers could not have exploded.

Divers who have been down to the wreck unanimously testify that the bow of the ship (where the ammunition was stored) was blasted by a massive internal (from the inside out) explosion.

[6] Mr. Isaac Lehmann of New York City made a sworn statement that he saw at least thirty people crushed to death by one of the lifeboats sliding across the deck.

*[Continued on next page.]*

*[Continued from previous page.]*

## Historian B (1975)

*(1)* People have traditionally felt that the German torpedo attack on the *Lusitania* on May 7, 1915, was morally wrong and deserved the condemnation of the world. But in 1975 Historian A burst on the scene with two articles and a book on the sensational theory that Britain was responsible for the disaster. It is unfortunate that so many people have believed Historian A's arguments since he is not a trained historian at all, but rather, a newspaper correspondent. His writing mingles history and historical fiction in a thoroughly misleading way.

*(2)* It is true that the *Lusitania* carried munitions on her voyage in May, that the British did arm some of their merchant ships with weapons to sink unsuspecting submarines, and that the Germans warned passengers in America that liners entering the war zone could be sunk. Nevertheless, the German U-boat commander was not morally justified in sinking the *Lusitania*. Over one thousand innocent civilians were killed. As President Wilson argued, to say the U-boat commander was not wrong is like saying that if a bloodthirsty killer warns his victims first, then the killer is not wrong.

*(3)* The Germans cried that it was wrong for the United States to trade munitions with her enemy, but not with her. The United States had no way to trade with Germany (because of the British blockade), so the situation could not be avoided. It has been a common practice for neutrals to sell arms to one side in a war while not being able to sell to the other side. Germany herself had sold arms to the British during the Boer War, while not selling to the Boers due to the British naval blockade.[1]

*(4)* Historian A argues that the *Lusitania* was to be met by the warship *Juno* and escorted to port. There is no evidence, however, to show that the *Juno* was ever ordered to meet the *Lusitania*. It would have been illogical to order the slower cruiser to escort the swift liner—the *Juno* would only have slowed down the *Lusitania*. The cruiser would have been ineffective against the submarine, serving only as a second target.

*(5)* Historian A charges that the *Lusitania* was not warned of submarines in the area, but the evidence shows she was warned several times.[2]

*(6)* Historian A tries to make it look like First Lord of the Admiralty Winston Churchill planned to let the Germans sink the *Lusitania* to draw the United States into the war on England's side. Historian A's conspiracy theory is an illusion, as the two previous arguments show—there was never to be an escort and the ship was warned. Based on Winston Churchill's actions during the rest of his life, it is impossible to believe that he would deliberately leave civilians to die.

*(7)* Historian A makes another ridiculous argument when he says that the ammunition on board exploded, causing the ship to sink so fast. The problem with this argument is that the torpedo hit the ship between the first and second boiler rooms, some 150 feet from where the ammunition was stored.[3] Surely, the torpedo could not cause the munitions to explode at that distance, especially when repeated testing shows that even in a fire, small arms ammunition does not explode, it just shoots

*[Continued on next page.]*

## Historian B

*[Continued from previous page.]*

off like fireworks.[4] Also, no passenger testified to smelling the acrid odor of exploding munitions.

(8) Historian A argues that the ship was loaded with gun cotton which explodes when it contacts ocean water. Why would the British put gun cotton, which they desperately needed, on a ship which they were hoping would be sunk? Moreover *tightly packed* gun cotton will not explode when contacted with salt water.

(9) The finding by deep sea diver John Light[5] of an outward rip in the sunken *Lusitania,* on the opposite side (the port side) from where the torpedo hit (the starboard side), confirms the most logical explanation of what happened— a boiler exploded. The nineteen boilers of the *Lusitania* were under 195 pounds per square inch of pressure, so upon impact they could easily explode.[6] Wesley Frost, United States consul at Queenstown in 1915, wrote a book listing eighteen steamships that suffered bursting boilers after being torpedoed. He concluded that at least half of all steamships torpedoed sank in ten minutes or less.[7] Thus the eighteen-minute sinking of the *Lusitania* doesn't seem so extraordinary.

(10) Historian A incorrectly blames the extensive loss of life on the design of the *Lusitania*, charging that the longitudinal design caused the ship to list, preventing many lifeboats from being launched. The designer of a passenger liner, however, cannot be asked to design a ship with a torpedo attack in mind. The *Lusitania* was designed to stay afloat with damage caused by ordinary maritime hazards (such as icebergs and storms).

(11) When the *Lusitania* was sinking, the *Juno* was sent out to rescue survivors and then recalled, as Historian A says. It should be noted, however, that the original order to send the *Juno* out violated Admiralty policy. Many warships, such as the *Cressy* and *Hogue*, had been sunk while trying to rescue survivors. The *Juno* would have been another sitting duck for torpedo attack. Admiral Coke only recalled the *Juno* when he learned that fourteen other ships were moving to the area. Moreover, the *Juno* was not within sight of the passengers when it was ordered to turn around.

(12) At the inquiry into the sinking of the *Lusitania,* the British Admiralty found that Captain Turner bore a lot of the responsibility. He had been warned four times that there were submarines in the area, but he failed to sail in midchannel, operate at full speed (he was going only 18 knots), or follow a zigzag course.[8] Had Captain Turner been in midchannel (rather than closer to shore where the ship was a better target), he would have missed the U-boat; had he steered a zigzag course, he would have dodged the torpedo.

(13) The *Lusitania* sinking did not happen the way Historian A described. The liner was not used by the British Admiralty to draw the United States into World War I; it did not sink because the ammunition on board exploded; and the British did not cover up the sinking in the following investigation. The truth about the *Lusitania* shows the dangers of untrained amateurs trying to write history.

*[Continued on next page.]*

*[Continued from previous page.]*

## *Endnotes for Historian B*

[1] Evidence of Germany trading with the British during the Boer War is contained in *Papers Relating to the Foreign Relations of the United States*, 1915 Supplement, (Washington, 1915), p. 795.

[2] The British Admiralty sent a wireless message to the *Lusitania* on the morning of May 7, 1915, that submarines were active in the southern part of the Irish Channel. Public Records Office, British Admiralty Files, 137/105, Frames 28–29 (Valencia Log).

[3] The location at which the torpedo struck the ship comes from the testimony of survivors of the *Lusitania*. Note in the drawing below how far the torpedo hit from the ammunition (about 150 feet) and the direct damage to the two boiler rooms.

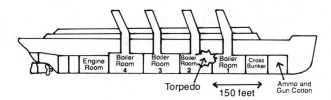

[4] Carlton Savage, *Policy of the United States toward Maritime Commerce in War* (Washington, 1936) II, p. 335. Extensive field tests, including the burning of boxes of ammunition in open fires, showed that munitions do not explode in one large explosion.

[5] Kenneth MacLeigh, "Was There a Gun?" *Sports Illustrated*, XVII (December 24, 1962), p. 37. This article describes Light's findings.

[6] When the *Lusitania* neared Liverpool, England, on February 5, 1915, Captain Dow said that he feared that his ship, if hit in the boilers by a torpedo, would be destroyed.

[7] Wesley Frost, *German Submarine Warfare* (New York, 1918), Chapters IV, V.

[8] One warning read, "Avoid headlands [the coastlands]; pass harbours at full speed; steer midchannel course. Submarines off Fastnet [a marker off the coast of Ireland near where the *Lusitania* was sunk]."

## Survey: Contraband and Submarines

 Suppose you are the leader of an island nation which is at war. Your enemy is using submarines to stop merchant ships which are delivering badly needed supplies to your country. Currently the submarines are surfacing, stopping the ships, letting people off, and then sinking the ships. Which of the following would you do?

| | Option | Would do | Would not do | Reasons why you would or would not do this |
|---|---|---|---|---|
| 1 | Arm your merchant ships so that they can sink submarines when the subs surface. | | | |
| 2 | Tell the captains of your merchant ships to ram submarines when they surface. (This will not damage the ships since they are much larger than the subs.) | | | |
| 3 | Put ammunition and other war armaments (called contraband) on passenger ships. These ships have the citizens of other countries on them. | | | |
| 4 | Tell the captains of your merchant ships to fly the flags of neutral countries. The submarine commanders may think the ships are not yours. | | | |

*[Continued on next page.]*

*[Continued from previous page.]*

 Suppose you are the leader of a country which is at war with an island nation. Your enemy controls the ocean with its large navy and is causing starvation in your country with its blockade. You have submarines which could cut off delivery of supplies to your enemy. The enemy has, however, sunk several of your subs when they have surfaced to warn passengers and crew before torpedoing the ships. Which of the following would you do?

| | Option | Would do | Would not do | Reasons why you would or would not do this |
|---|---|---|---|---|
| 5 | Use submarines to sink merchant ships of your enemy, but not if passengers from neutral countries are thought to be on them. | | | |
| 6 | Use submarines to sink passenger ships of your enemy, even if some of the passengers are from neutral countries. | | | |
| 7 | Order the submarines to surface, warn the ships, and let all passengers and crew off the ships before sinking them. | | | |

## LESSON 9      Why Did the United States Enter World War I?

## Background Information

This lesson presents two viewpoints of the main reason the United States entered World War I. This is not the same question as what caused the war itself. It has nothing to do with the assassination of the Archduke Ferdinand, for example. The dates in parentheses next to the historians are the publication dates of the original interpretation.

---

### Historian A (1934)

*(1)* In August 1914 the State Department stated publicly that American bank loans to the governments at war in Europe would not be neutral; they would put the United States on the side of the Allies (England and France). Later, the State Department got around its own statement by using a trick. The State Department, in October 1914, said that credits (which is just another name for loans) were different from loans and that it was all right for American banks, especially J. P. Morgan Bank, to give credits to the warring countries.

*(2)* As soon as the credits were made, the Allies used them to buy American goods to fight the war. Since Germany could not buy American goods (because of the British blockade), the United States was now helping the Allies, but not Germany. That is, the United States was not neutral anymore.

*(3)* War trade with the Allies resulted in great prosperity for the United States—business profits were high, the gross national product was expanding, and unemployment was down. The United States was dependent on England and France for its prosperity, and this dependence made us unneutral. For example, we did not protest violations by England, our largest customer, of our neutral rights at sea, while we loudly protested German violations of our rights.

*(4)* Other historians have argued that the main cause for the United States entry into World War I was the German submarine campaign. That argument leaves out the fact that United States loans and supplies to the Allies already made us enemies of Germany, so we really forced Germany to use the submarines. Even the German decision to start unrestricted submarine warfare (the event which some argue led directly to the United States declaration of war) was forced by the United States. The United States was already completely involved in the war except for sending troops, and the Allies, backed by American economic power, would have defeated Germany anyway. The Germans took a gamble on their one chance for victory—it shortened the war, but it did not change the outcome.

*(5)* President Wilson's words show that, even in his view, granting loans made us unneutral and forced us into World War I. He stated in April 1915 that "in the judgment of this government, loans by American bankers to any foreign nation which is at war, are inconsistent with the true spirit of neutrality." As was shown above, the government later allowed American

*[Continued on next page.]*

---

## Historian A

*[Continued from previous page.]*

bankers to make such loans. The fact that we changed the name from loans to credits made no difference—they still put us firmly on the Allied side.

(6) German submarines were not the main reason for the United States en-try into World War I. Rather, United States loans and trade with the Allies forced the Germans to use unrestricted submarine warfare to stop aid from a country (the United States) which was already her enemy.

## Historian B (1935, 1954)

(1) Recent viewpoints of the causes of American intervention in World War I have brought up many factors. There is the suggestion by some historians of loans and the greed of United States capitalists. There is talk by other historians of propaganda and sympathy for the Allies, and even a change in the balance of power in Europe if Germany won. None of these factors, however, shows how the United States might have stayed at peace—none conclusively shows why we went to war.

(2) Dominant sentiment in the United States was certainly pro-Ally. American economic prosperity depended upon the maintenance of our trade with the Allies. But it is a far cry from these facts to the assumption that because of them we adopted a policy which led us into war. It would be necessary to show that emotional sympathy and material interests overcame the strong pacifistic sentiment (feelings against war) of Congress and the people. It would be necessary to show that these factors pushed Wilson to declare war over his own pacifist sentiments.

(3) Wilson was sympathetic toward the Allies, but he also tried very hard to prevent that feeling from affecting United States policy. He protested not only German violations of American neutral rights at sea, but also British violations. He sent notes of protest to England and, in the summer of 1916, secured wide powers from Congress permitting him to prohibit loans and to impose embargoes, if necessary, to counter British violations. United States actions against Britain were limited because the country's economic interests lay with continuing the munitions trade, but this only limited our quarrel with England. It does not show why we went to war against Germany.

(4) The German submarine campaign was the reason for United States entrance into the war. So long as the German government stuck to her *Sussex* pledge (a pledge not to attack unarmed neutral ships), Wilson would have continued his neutral course. America would have continued her protest against British interference with American trade. "If Germany had not alienated American sympathies," wrote Colonel House (advisor to Wilson), "by her mode of warfare, the United States would not have put up with Allied control of American trade on the high seas." Submarines were far different in effect than surface ships. Submarines sank ships and killed people, while surface ships stopped neutral vessels and seized illegal cargoes. The submarine campaign, unlike

*[Continued on next page.]*

## Historian B

*[Continued from previous page.]*

the Allied blockade, involved indiscriminate destruction of American property. It permitted no distinction between contraband (war goods) and free goods.

(5) It is inexact to state that our export of munitions forced the Germans to adopt submarine warfare and drew us into the war. All the evidence available shows that even without American export of munitions to the Allies, the Germans would have utilized the unrestricted submarine campaign as the only effective means of striking at Great Britain.

(6) It is still further from the truth to state that our intervention was determined by pressure from financial groups which had acquired a vast stake in the fortunes of the Allies. Whether the Allies won the war or not, that stake was largely secure. Moreover, the businessmen and bankers with this stake had no means of exercising pressure upon the President or upon Congress. We know as a historical fact that no effective pressure was exercised.

(7) By raising the submarine issue at critical moments from 1915 on, Ger-

many herself made it difficult or impossible for America to protest British infractions of our right to trade freely. It was the Germans who had alternatives available to them—they could accept Wilson's leadership in the peace program; they could continue their submarine campaign as it was; or they could try the desperate gamble of unrestricted submarine warfare. They chose the third alternative in hopes of dominating Europe, if not the world.

(8) It was the German decision for unrestricted submarine warfare, alone, which forced Wilson to take steps for war. American ships were being sunk and American citizens were being killed on the high seas. Considerations of America's alleged economic stake in an Allied victory did not influence Wilson's thoughts during the critical weeks from February 1 to April 2, 1917, nor did considerations of national interest or the great ideological issues at stake in the conflict.

(9) Without the submarine campaign, we would not have entered the war, no matter what other circumstances there were.

 **Historian A**

1. What is the main point of Historian A's argument?

*[Continued on next page.]*

*[Continued from previous page.]*

2. What is an unstated assumption in the last sentence in paragraph 3?

3. What is an unstated assumption in paragraph 2, sentences two and three?

4. What is the fallacy in the second to last sentence in paragraph 4?

    _____ A. Appeal to the Golden Mean (p. 13)

    _____ B. Straw Man (p. 14)

    _____ C. False Scenario (p. 6)

    _____ D. Hasty Generalization (p. 10)

    _____ E. Negative Proof (p. 12)

5. Evaluate the reasoning used in:

    a. The first sentence of paragraph 3

    b. The second sentence of paragraph 3

    c. The third sentence of paragraph 4

6. Evaluate the evidence used in the second sentence of paragraph 5.

*[Continued on next page.]*

*[Continued from previous page.]*

 **Historian B**

7. What is the main point of Historian B's argument?


8. What is the unstated assumption in paragraph 4, the sentence that begins, "Submarines sank ships...?"


9. What is the fallacy in the second sentence of paragraph 4?


10. What is the fallacy in the second sentence of paragraph 5 (also in paragraph 9)?


11. What is the fallacy in the first sentence of paragraph 8?


12. List one word from the second sentence of paragraph 1 and one word from the second to last sentence in paragraph 4 which make a value judgment.


13. List a total of two unclear (or undefined) words in the second sentence of paragraph 3, the second sentence of paragraph 5, and the first sentence of paragraph 7.


*[Continued on next page.]*

*[Continued from previous page.]*

14. One of the types of reasoning which historians use to reach their conclusions is debating. How well do you think Historian B does in showing that the following arguments are wrong?

   a.   Allied propaganda and American sympathy for the Allies were the cause for the United States entry into World War I.

   b.   American loans and war trade drew the United States into World War I.

15. Assume that Historian B showed conclusively that Allied propaganda and American loans and trade were not important factors in drawing the United States into the War. How well does Historian B show that the main cause he argues for *did* push the United States into the War?

 **General Question**

16. Is Historian A or Historian B's viewpoint stronger? Why do you think so?

## LESSON 10      Identifying and Evaluating Evidence

### Identifying Evidence

**Q** Label each item below with the appropriate letter.

    **S**    A **source** of information is given.

    **N**    **No** source of information is given.

_____1.    In May and June 1989, Chinese soldiers opened fire on civilian protesters in Tiananmen Square, killing many of them.

_____2.    The 1988 fire in Yellowstone Park burned about a million acres, almost half of the entire park.

_____3.    Amnesty International, a human rights organization, reported that human rights workers in Guatemala received death threats and were held by three men belonging to the Guatemalan armed forces.

_____4.    Though most Americans admired the technological advances of the 1920s, some were distressed by their challenge to the ways of the "good old days."

_____5.    Charles Lindbergh became a hero to millions of Americans in the 1920s when he made the first solo transatlantic flight to France.

_____6.    Hiram Wesley Evans, the "Imperial Wizard" of the Ku Klux Klan, wrote in a 1926 article that the Klan represented the Nordic race, and that race alone.

_____7.    Women, in much larger numbers than in the past, smoked cigarettes in the 1920s, as shown in a 1920 *New York Times* article, "Women Smokers."

### Evaluating Evidence

**Q** Evaluate the following pieces of evidence by listing the strengths and weaknesses of each. If you need help, refer to the section on **Evidence** in the "Guide to Critical Thinking" (Unit 1).

8. Historian Frederick Lewis Allen says in his book, *Only Yesterday*, published in 1931, that Secretary of the Interior Bernard Fall secretly leased the Teapot Dome oil reserves to an oil company, and personally received from the company's

*[Continued on next page.]*

*[Continued from previous page.]*

owner $260,000 in bonds. Allen says this shows Fall made an illegal deal with the oil company.

STRENGTHS:                          WEAKNESSES:

9. We want to know what Franklin Roosevelt's goals were in his New Deal Program. We find his 1933 inaugural address stating that the government will help put people to work through needed projects, raise the price for crops, unify relief activities for the poor, regulate banking, and stabilize the money supply.

STRENGTHS:                          WEAKNESSES:

10. We want to know whether the police or striking workers started the violence at the Chicago Republic Steel Plant on May 30, 1937. We find a *New York Times* article from the same day entitled "4 Killed, 84 Hurt as Strikers Fight Police in Chicago: Steel Mob Halted." The article states, "The police said they stood their ground but made no effort to harm the invaders until showered with bricks and bolts....When the rioters resorted to firearms, the police said, they were forced to draw their revolvers to protect themselves."

STRENGTHS:                          WEAKNESSES:

11. On the same topic of the Republic Steel Plant violence (Question 10), we find a Senate Subcommittee Report on a film taken by Paramount Pictures at the scene of the confrontation between police and strikers. The report says that the film shows a line of strikers facing a line of policemen while the head of the strikers and policemen argue. "Then suddenly, without apparent warning, there is a terrific roar of pistol shots, and men in the front ranks of the marchers (strikers) go down like grass before a scythe....The massive sustained roar of the police pistols lasts perhaps two or three seconds....Instantly the police charge on the marchers with riot sticks flying."

STRENGTHS:                          WEAKNESSES:

# LESSON 11     Identifying and Evaluating Comparisons

## Identifying Comparisons

An item might involve a comparison as well as some other type of reasoning, such as cause and effect. If so, label it **C**. If you need help, look at the section on **Comparisons** in the "Guide to Critical Thinking" (Unit 1).

**Q**   Label each item below with the appropriate letter.

     **C**   The item involves **comparison** reasoning.

     **N**   The item does **not** involve comparison reasoning.

_____1.   I went to the public library because it is better than our school library.

_____2.   Four kids on our street went to camp this summer.

_____3.   I enjoy playing basketball in my spare time because I like the exercise and competition.

_____4.   Ronald Reagan was to the 1980s what Calvin Coolidge was to the 1920s. They were both pro-business and served in an era of prosperity.

_____5.   Governor Calvin Coolidge took strong action against the strikers in the 1920 Boston Police Strike.

_____6.   More cars were produced per year in the 1920s than in previous years.

_____7.   Franklin D. Roosevelt, because of his brilliant political skills and his willingness to experiment, was a much better president than was Herbert Hoover.

_____8.   The Agricultural Adjustment Act was an important part of the New Deal.

## Evaluating Comparisons

> The key question for evaluating comparisons is
>
> • How are the two cases similar and how are they different?

**Q**   Use this question to evaluate each comparison below. In general, the more similarities, the better the comparison.

9. Due to greater factory output, advertising increased greatly in the 1920s. In 1929, for example, more that $3 billion was spent on advertising, compared to about $1 billion per year before World War I.

*[Continued on next page.]*

*[Continued from previous page.]*

10. Farmers were getting poorer in the 1920s. The prices they received for their crops were going down steadily while the cost of taxes, farm implements, fuel, clothes, and other products they had to buy were going up.

11. The New Deal was successful in helping the economy recover from its collapse, as shown by unemployment figures. In 1933, when the New Deal began, there were 12.8 million people unemployed. By 1937 the number of people unemployed had dropped to 7.7 million.

12. Use the statistics below to argue, contrary to the argument in item 11, that unemployment figures show the New Deal was not successful.

## Unemployment, 1929–1939 (in thousands)

| Year | Total Labor Force | Number Unemployed | Percent |
|------|-------------------|-------------------|---------|
| 1929 | 49,180 | 1,550 | 3.2 |
| 1930 | 49,820 | 4,340 | 8.7 |
| 1931 | 50,420 | 8,020 | 15.9 |
| 1932 | 51,000 | 12,060 | 23.6 |
| 1933 | 51,590 | 12,830 | 24.9 |
| 1934 | 52,230 | 11,340 | 21.7 |
| 1935 | 52,870 | 10,610 | 20.1 |
| 1936 | 53,440 | 9,030 | 16.9 |
| 1937 | 54,000 | 7,700 | 14.3 |
| 1938 | 54,610 | 10,390 | 19.0 |
| 1939 | 55,230 | 9,480 | 17.2 |

# LESSON 12      Analyzing Cause and Effect

## Connection Between Cause and Effect

The Eighteenth Amendment, ratified (approved) in 1919, outlawed the sale of beer, wine, and distilled liquors beginning in January 1920. The Volstead Act was passed to enforce the amendment. This was the beginning of Prohibition (manufacture, sale, or transportation of alcohol was illegal). It lasted until 1933.

This part of the lesson consists of three viewpoints, all of which argue that Prohibition led to a tremendous increase in organized crime, also referred to as the mob, gangsters, racketeers, etc.

 Read the three viewpoints, then choose which viewpoint is strongest and tell why you think so. The key question to be answered here is "How well does each historian explain the connection between the cause and the effect?"

### Historian A

Prohibition led to a tremendous increase in organized crime in the 1920s. With the sale of alcohol illegal, the supply shrank. But millions of people still wanted to drink, so the price skyrocketed. According to reporter Ernest Mandeville, the profit from sales of "needle beer" (illegal, home-brewed beer) in Detroit in 1925 was 1000%. The mob was ideally suited to fill the demand for alcohol. After all, there was no legal competition. Fueled by such easy money, organized crime spread quickly.

### Historian B

Prohibition led to a tremendous increase in organized crime in the 1920s. Supporters of Prohibition were generally small town, farming Protestants, while the opposition drew its strength from urban groups of mixed religious affiliation who believed in a more secular (worldly) outlook and a freer life-style. This latter group, which comprised a large minority, or even a majority, of the American public, refused to obey the Volstead Act. Organized crime naturally spread from this opposition. According to a 1929 article in *Harper's Monthly*, racketeering cost consumers plenty of money, especially in Chicago.

*[Continued on next page.]*

*[Continued from previous page.]*

> ## Historian C
>
> Prohibition led to a tremendous increase in organized crime in the 1920s. After the Volstead Act was passed, smugglers brought whiskey in across the Canadian border, or on fast boats from the Caribbean. To supplement the supplies of these "rum-runners," there were countless home distillers of illicit whiskey, much of it bad and some of it poisonous. It was easy to buy whiskey by the case, the bottle, or the drink. Indeed, "speakeasies" (illegal saloons) did business in every major city, and obliging policemen and cab drivers were glad to tell strangers where they were. Naturally, in such an atmosphere, the mob grew and with it the level of violence. The number of bombings increased from 51 in 1920, to 92 in 1924, to 116 in 1928 (from "The High Cost of Hoodlums," *Harpers Monthly Magazine*, October 1929, p. 529).

1.  Which of the three viewpoints is strongest? Why do you think so?

    (This question is asking "Which argument makes the strongest connection between the cause and the effect?")

## Identifying Cause-and-Effect Arguments

To be cause-and-effect reasoning, the statement has to argue that something caused, led to, or brought about something else.

**Q** Label each of the following with the appropriate letter. For those items that you identify as cause-and-effect reasoning, write the cause and the effect in the space provided.

> **C** Item illustrates **cause-and-effect** reasoning.
>
> **N** Item does **not** illustrate cause-and-effect reasoning.

_____ 2.  Bill drives his car to work, except on Fridays when he walks.

CAUSE:                          EFFECT:

*[Continued on next page.]*

*[Continued from previous page.]*

_____3. The family had to pay $600 to fix the car, so they were forced to cancel their trip.

CAUSE:                                    EFFECT:

_____4. Industrialization in the 1920s brought more leisure time to masses of people.

CAUSE:                                    EFFECT:

_____5. The wave of labor strikes after World War I, and the founding of the Communist Party, triggered an anti-radicalism reaction in the United States known as the Red Scare.

CAUSE:                                    EFFECT:

_____6. In 1928 President Herbert Hoover could talk about the possibility of ending poverty without fear of being ridiculed.

CAUSE:                                    EFFECT:

_____7. The flapper—the new woman of the 1920s—asked for the same social freedom that men enjoyed.

CAUSE:                                    EFFECT:

## LESSON 13     Were Sacco and Vanzetti Guilty?

## Sorting Information by Point of View

At 3:00 p.m. on April 15, 1920, Frederick Parmenter, paymaster at the Slator and Morrill Shoe Company of Braintree, Massachusetts, and Allessandro Berardelli, his guard, were murdered while taking the $15,776.51 payroll from the company's office to the factory. Two suspects, Nicola Sacco and Bartolomeo Vanzetti, were arrested and charged with the murder.

**Q** Label each item below with the appropriate letter.

**G**  Item could be used to show that Sacco and Vanzetti were **guilty**.

**I**  Item could be used to show that they were **innocent.**

**N**  Item could **not** be used to show their guilt or innocence.

_____1.  Witnesses said the crime was committed by a gang of four or five men.

_____2.  The killers were identified as Italians by some witnesses, and Sacco and Vanzetti were Italians.

_____3.  A similar crime was committed before this one, in Bridgewater, Massachusetts. There were gangs involved in both crimes. Each gang had a car, and in both cases the gang members were identified as Italians.

_____4.  Sacco and Vanzetti were part of a gang and one of the gang members, named Boda, had a car.

_____5.  When arrested, Sacco and Vanzetti were very nervous and they were armed with guns.

_____6.  Sacco and Vanzetti lied to the police about why they went to get Boda's car and why they were armed when they were arrested.

_____7.  The gang to which Sacco and Vanzetti belonged believed in anarchism, that is, the radical idea that the government should be abolished. They claimed to be pacifists (people opposed to violence). They were against the United States government.

_____8.  When Sacco and Vanzetti were arrested, they were dragged to the police station without being told what the charges were against them.

_____9.  Sacco and Vanzetti said they were afraid anarchists were being persecuted (unjustly treated) by police and they felt no one would believe they were armed to protect themselves at the time they were arrested.

*[Continued on next page.]*

*[Continued from previous page.]*

_____10. Vanzetti had already been convicted of a similar crime (armed robbery) in Bridgewater, Massachusetts.

_____11. The police stopped their investigation after Sacco and Vanzetti were arrested.

_____12. Two of the other men in the gang, Boda and Orciani, had alibis. That is, they gave evidence that they were somewhere else when the crime was committed.

_____13. Witnesses at the scene of the crime said it happened too fast to make positive identifications.

_____14. At the police station some witnesses identified Sacco, while other witnesses identified Anthony Palmisano who was in jail at the time of the crime.

_____15. The judge in the case, Webster Thayer, wanted radicals put in jail.

_____16. At the trial, seven witnesses positively identified Sacco and four witnesses identified Vanzetti as having committed the crime. All of these witnesses were upstanding citizens who had nothing to gain by lying. None of the witnesses was completely sure, however, that Sacco or Vanzetti were the men. One witness's identification of Sacco was thrown out because he had made contradictory statements to four other people. Another witness identified Sacco in the car as it was traveling about 20 miles per hour. A witness who identified Vanzetti was shown to not have seen anyone in the car—he had ducked out of fear of being shot.

_____17. Descriptions of the bandits varied considerably among the witnesses at first. Some witnesses described the criminals as light-skinned with blonde hair. Others described the bandits as dark-skinned and dark-haired. The latter characteristics fit Sacco and Vanzetti.

_____18. One witness who identified Sacco at the trial said, when first questioned by police, that she could not make a positive identification. She said the suspect she saw had large hands, but Sacco had rather small hands.

_____19. Witnesses were called into jail before the trial, shown pictures of Sacco and Vanzetti, and asked if these men were the criminals. No police line-up was used.

_____20. Some witnesses said the men they saw at the scene of the crime were not Sacco and Vanzetti.

_____21. Captain John Proctor of the State Police fired 14 test bullets through Sacco's gun and compared them to Bullet III—the bullet that killed Berardelli. Bullet III was an obsolete type (no longer being manufactured)

*[Continued on next page.]*

*[Continued from previous page.]*

with a milled groove in it. (Sacco had six such bullets on him at the police station.) Proctor used similar bullets. When the prosecutor asked Proctor if Bullet III was fired from Sacco's Colt automatic he replied, "My opinion is that it is consistent with being fired by that pistol." He also said that the indentation made by the firing pin on Shell W, found at the scene of the murders, and the test shells fired in Sacco's gun were consistent with being fired from the same weapon.

_____ 22. Charles Van Amburgh worked at the Remington Union Metallic Cartridge Company of Bridgeport, Connecticut. Before working at Remington he had spent nine years at the Springfield Arsenal and at Westinghouse and Colt Firearms. By measuring bands he determined that Bullet III was fired from a .32–caliber Colt. On the witness stand he said, "I am inclined to believe that it was fired, Number III bullet was fired, from this Colt automatic pistol." A rough rust track at the bottom of the barrel corresponded to marks on the bullet. Under cross examination he agreed that it is common for Colts to rust on the bottom of the barrels.

_____ 23. Several witnesses said Vanzetti was in Plymouth all day on April 15, 1920. It was a year later when they said this, but they each remembered the day well because something significant had happened to them that day.

_____ 24. Several witnesses, including Giuseppe Andraver a clerk at the Italian consulate, stated that Sacco was in Boston all day on April 15, 1920. Though it was a year later when they said this, they remembered because there had been a big rally that night.

_____ 25. All witnesses to Sacco and Vanzetti's locations in Boston and Plymouth on the day of the crime were Italian immigrants, and many were friends of Sacco and Vanzetti.

_____ 26. Celestino Madeiros, who was under indictment for murder, confessed to the Braintree slayings. He said that he and others from the Morelli gang of Providence, Rhode Island were involved. He gave a lot of factual details about the crime. Joe Morelli, the gang leader, looked like Sacco, and he owned the same type of gun that Sacco did, a Colt .32. Five other bullets found at the scene of the crime came from the same type of gun owned by Tony Mancini, another Morelli gang member.

_____ 27. Madeiros shared a jail cell with Sacco. Soon after the crime, Madeiros deposited a sum of money which was close to what his cut of the money from the robbery would have been.

_____ 28. A cap of roughly the same size as one found in Sacco's kitchen was found at the scene of the crime. Sacco's employer identified the cap as being similar in color and appearance to the one that he had seen Sacco wearing.

*[Continued on next page.]*

*[Continued from previous page.]*

_____29. A historian had Sacco's pistol retested in 1961. Because of the markings on the shells, he concluded that Sacco's gun fired the fatal shot.

_____30. In 1988 Charlie Whipple wrote an article in the *Boston Globe* about an encounter he had in 1937 with ballistic expert Sgt. Edward Seibolt. Seibolt told Whipple that he had worked on the Sacco-Vanzetti case. He said that "we switched the murder weapon in that case" because "we suspected the other side [defense] of switching weapons, so we just switched them back." Seibolt said he would call Whipple a liar if he printed the story, so Whipple did not print it for 51 years.

_____31. Years after the trial, Albert H. Hamilton, a ballistics expert of 15 years, conducted tests on the fatal bullet and a test bullet from Sacco's gun and concluded, based on differences in markings, that the fatal bullet did not go through Sacco's gun. Augustus H. Gill, a professor of technical chemical analysis at MIT, also did tests and concluded the fatal bullet was not fired from Sacco's gun.

_____32. According to the notes of the assistant district attorney (prosecution), three shell casings were found at the scene of the crime. The jury was shown four shells. Only one of the shells was proved to have been fired through Sacco's gun.

_____33. The cap at the scene of the crime was black and had earflaps. A cap brought from Sacco's house was grey and did not have earflaps.

_____34. James Burns was a ballistics engineer with the U.S. Cartridge Company for 30 years. He said Bullet III could have been fired from a Colt automatic but also from a different type of gun called a Bayard. When asked by the defense attorney if Bullet III was fired from Sacco's gun, he responded, "In my opinion, no. It doesn't compare at all."

_____35. J. Henry Fitzgerald worked for 28 years in the weapons business and was in charge of the testing room at the Colt Patent Firearms Company at the time of the trial. He testified that, "Number III Bullet was not fired from the Sacco pistol. I can see no pitting or marks on bullet Number III that would correspond with a bullet coming from this gun."

_____36. According to one historian, by 1961 the barrel of the Sacco pistol would have rusted so much that any test done with it would not have been reliable. The experts who tested it said they cleaned it out by firing two preliminary rounds through the barrel. This would have changed the inside of the barrel. Further, in 1924 a district attorney claimed the gun barrel of Sacco's gun had been switched with another new Colt automatic used in test firings. Judge Thayer had the barrels switched back. So it is unclear whether after 1929 the barrel was the real one.

*[Continued on next page.]*

*[Continued from previous page.]*

_____37. Sacco and his attorney agreed to have test bullets fired from his pistol to see if it was the murder weapon. The testimony by ballistics experts at the trial (#21, 22, 34, 35) was all based on those test firings.

_____38. Fred Loring said he found the cap at the scene of the crime 18 inches from Berardelli's body immediately after the shooting. Actually, he found it in the middle of the street on the evening of April 16, almost 30 hours after the robbery. The prosecuting attorneys knew Loring was lying but let him testify anyway.

_____39. In a sworn statement made in October 1923, Captain John Proctor said that what he meant in his testimony at the Sacco-Vanzetti Trial (#21) was that Bullet III had been fired by a Colt automatic, not that it had been fired by Sacco's Colt automatic, and that the questions asked him at Dedham were carefully framed to make it appear he thought Sacco was guilty when he didn't necessarily think so.

## Arguing the Case

 Now look back over the information and decide whether you think Sacco and Vanzetti actually committed the crime (not whether they should be found guilty or not guilty in court, but whether they committed the crime). Then take the information that favors your point of view and write an argument here.

*[Continued on next page.]*

*[Continued from previous page.]*

 What impression does this photograph give you of Sacco and Vanzetti (the two men in the middle)? How might photographs be used by the prosecution or defense to influence a jury?

Library of Congress Collection

## LESSON 14     What Caused the Great Depression?

### Glossary of Terms on the Depression

The Great Depression, which began in late 1929 and lasted until roughly 1940, was the worst depression in American history. Historians disagree sharply on the main cause of the depression. Since the topic is quite complicated, you need to have a clear understanding of the terms involved in order to evaluate the arguments.

**Banking Panic**  A situation in which many bank depositors withdraw their money (called a run on the bank) causing a large number of banks to close.

**Bull Market**  A situation in which the prices of stocks rise significantly.

**Consumption**  Spending money to purchase or buy goods and services.

**Depression**  A dramatic slowdown in the economy, characterized by a significant decline in the Gross National Product (GNP) and national income, and a great increase in unemployment.

**Federal Reserve Bank**  An independent government agency which controls, through various procedures, the supply of money. It also has significant influence over interest rates.

**Gross National Product**  The measure of all the goods and services produced in a country in one year, measured in dollars in the United States.

**Interest Rates**  The amount charged for borrowing money. Many businesses borrow money to expand their output. Thus, higher interest rates can slow down business (and economic) growth, and lower interest rates can lead to business growth.

**Money**  Currency (paper money and coins) plus demand deposits (checking accounts)—most money is in the form of checking accounts, not currency.

**National Income**  The total net income earned in production of goods and services. It is the same as Gross National Product except that it does not include things such as allowances for wear and tear on machinery and buildings.

**Production**  The making of goods or performance of services.

**Recession**  A mild slowdown in the economy, less dramatic than a depression.

**Speculation**  Buying a product with the hope that the product can be sold later at a higher price.

**Stock Crash**  A dramatic drop in the price of stocks.

*[Continued on next page.]*

*[Continued from previous page.]*
## Relevant Information

 Use the relevant information below, read the viewpoints, and answer the questions which follow.

A. One economist estimates that total stock market investment was a very small percentage of the whole economy (between 1% and 2% of total national income).

B. National income declined by 36% from 1929 to 1933.

C. The richest 5% in America increased its share of income from 24% of total national income in 1922 to 26% of total national income in 1929.

D. There have been numerous bank panics and stock crashes in the United States. Some have been followed by depressions and some have not.

E. In any economy which is changing, there will be growing industries and declining industries.

F. Short-term interest rates declined dramatically after the stock market crash and remained low in 1930. Long-term rates on government securities stayed about the same. Long-term private interest rates went up.

G. Output of goods and services in 1933 was 50% below what it could have been, according to one economist.

### Historian A

When the stock crash took place in the last months of 1929, America plunged into its worst depression ever. The seeds of the depression lay in the seemingly prosperous American economy of the 1920s. Although the economy expanded in the '20s, there were a number of weaknesses in it.

First, there were several weak industries in the 1920s, notably agriculture, textiles, and coal mining. Second, there was the phenomenon of technological unemployment. With more machines used to make goods, some workers were laid off. The result was that although employment increased in the 1920s, it did not increase fast enough to keep up with population growth. Even in the best years of the 1920s there were 1.5 million people unemployed. Third, the income of the country was concentrated more in the hands of the wealthy. The poor people did not share equally in the prosperity of the 1920s. Fourth, Americans experienced numerous foreign trade problems, especially with Europe, in the 1920s.

### Historian B

The economic collapse of 1929, known as the Great Depression, was caused by several weaknesses in the American economy of the 1920s. These weaknesses included the decline of certain industries (especially agriculture), technological unemployment, and

*[Continued on next page.]*

## Historian B

*[Continued from previous page.]*

foreign trade problems. The most important weakness in the economy was the unequal distribution of income in the 1920s. Although wages went up during the decade, business profits went up much faster. Since profits and the income of rich people are used largely to produce goods, and since wages are used largely to consume goods, a situation of overproduction resulted. That is, more goods were produced than were being bought. Business started declining, which led to the stock collapse, and eventually to the Depression itself.

1. What is the main point of Historian A?

2. What is the main point of Historian B?

3. Which historian, A or B, gives a stronger explanation of unequal distribution of income as an important cause of the depression? Why do you think so?

4. What assumption do both Historians A and B make about the stock crash and the Depression?

5. Using the relevant information (p. 77) and your own thinking, show one weakness in:

   a. Historian A's viewpoint—

   b. Historian B's viewpoint—

*[Continued on next page.]*

*[Continued from previous page.]*

---

## Historian C

The 1929 stock crash obviously caused the Great Depression which followed it. There are three ways the crash contributed to the economic decline: 1. it reduced the money wealth of households, causing less spending; 2. it deprived business of an important way of raising money for investment (through stocks); and 3. it caused people to take a pessimistic view of the economy, thereby reducing investment. With spending and investment in decline, the economy had to decline.

---

## Historian D

It goes without saying that the 1929 stock crash caused the Great Depression. Throughout 1928 and 1929 people speculated on the great bull market. That is, they bought shares of stock on the gamble that the price of the stock would keep going up, rather than on the basis of the real value of the stock. The speculative boom was fueled by easy credit policies, especially buying on margin. Individuals could buy stocks on margin by putting down as little as 10 percent of the amount purchased and borrowing the other 90 percent from the stock broker. With people bidding on the stocks with borrowed money, stock prices soared. When prices declined in October 1929, many people had to sell fast in order to pay back their loans. Thus, the initial downturn in stock prices turned into a collapse.

---

6. Which historian, C or D, makes a stronger argument that the stock crash caused the Great Depression? Why do you think so?

7. Using the relevant information and your own thinking, show one weakness in Historian C's viewpoint.

---

## Historian E

In 1929 the American economy went into a recession. There is no need to explain why this occurred since the regular ups and downs of an economy cause periodic recessions as a matter of course. The important question is why the economy did not recover within a year as it usually does, but rather, plunged into the worst Depression in our history.

*[Continued on next page.]*

---

## Historian E

*[Continued from previous page.]*

The answer is that the supply of money shrank, causing less spending and thus higher unemployment. The money supply shrank first because there was a bank panic. People started withdrawing their deposits, and since bank deposits were not insured by the government (insured today by the FDIC), the other depositors removed their money before they lost it. As deposits were withdrawn, loans were called in and the money supply was drastically reduced.

Second, the Federal Reserve Bank took no action to stop the money supply from shrinking. In fact, in 1931, it actually took steps that made the supply of money even smaller! The money supply continued to decline up to 1933. By that time, it was 33 percent smaller than it had been in 1929. Notice how close that reduction is to the 36 percent drop in national income which occurred during the same four years.

As the supply of money shrank, people had less money with which to buy goods and services. Consequently, prices fell and fewer goods were sold. With fewer goods being sold, fewer goods were made, unemployment went up, and national income and GNP declined. The country was plunged into the Depression, not by businessmen, but by poor government policy in not protecting the banking industry, and by the foolish policy of the Federal Reserve Bank (a government agency) in reducing the money supply at the very time when the country needed a larger supply of money.

8. What is the main point of Historian E?

9. What is a possible weakness in Historian E's argument?

## Historian F

The stock market crash of 1929 was one factor that contributed to the Great Depression, but it was not an important factor. By reducing people's wealth, the crash caused a decline in spending, but the decline was not large enough to cause the tremendous drop in national income that occurred from 1929 to 1933.

The Depression was caused mainly by the dramatic decline in consumption in 1930. For some as yet unexplained reasons, buying declined greatly in 1930—the drop was five times as large as the 1929 drop.

The decline caused investments to fall. This decline in consumption also caused the decline in the supply of money, not the other way around. If

*[Continued on next page.]*

## Historian F

*[Continued from previous page.]*

the money supply had declined first, short-term interest rates would have been high (since the supply of money would have been smaller than the demand). But short-term interest rates were actually low, showing that the demand for money (due to less spending) was lower than the supply.

Other theories do not adequately show what primarily caused the Great Depression. The best explanation is the decline in spending during 1930.

10. What is Historian F's main point?

11. What is one question you would ask Historian F to better evaluate his viewpoint?

12. Using the relevant information and your own thinking, show one weakness in Historian F's viewpoint.

13. Based on the arguments they make on the causes of the Great Depression, what do you think each of the following would recommend to avoid or cure depressions?

    Historian B -

    Historian D -

    Historian E -

    Historian F -

14. Which viewpoint do you think is strongest? Why do you think so?

## LESSON 15     What Should Be Done to Cure the Depression?

It is 1933 and the United States is in the worst depression in its history. Unemployment is at an unbelievable 25% (8% unemployment is considered high), the Gross National Product is down, and businesses are going bankrupt in large numbers. You have just been elected president of the country. What will you do to cure the depression?

**Q** Below are ten proposals about what to do. Label your top choices 1, 2, 3 and the worst ideas 8, 9, 10. Leave the others blank.

_____1.  Government should plan our economy. With central planning by the government, the economy could grow without having periodic business depressions. Public goals, such as more economic equality, should, if necessary, be forced on businessmen.

_____2.  The government will restore public confidence in the economy by helping business. We should tax the rich businessmen less and the government should give subsidies (help such as tax breaks, research, grants of money etc. which saves businesses money) to businessmen. The businessmen will use this help to expand production; they will hire more workers, and the economy will get moving again. There should be a minimum of welfare for the poor as this drains off money from businesses.

_____3.  The government should get the businesses together and set up a planning agency (run by the government) to help businesses get going again. Within the agency, businesses would set up their own guidelines and regulations. For example, they could charge higher prices and they could cooperate rather than compete. The government would watch over the agency, but the businessmen would run the agency. Businessmen know best how to get business going again.

_____4.  The government must balance the budget. In this way government spending will be controlled. Almost all businessmen believe this is a healthy way to run both government and business. Thus, their confidence will be restored in the economy, they will expand production, and the economy will get moving again.

_____5.  The government must give much more welfare relief to the millions of people who are suffering from the Depression. It is the obligation of government to protect its poorer citizens from such suffering. The money to pay for welfare should come from heavier taxes on rich people. If the poor have more money, they will buy more products and business will be able to expand. In this way the country will get out of the Depression.

_____6.  To get out of the Depression, the government should deficit spend—that is, it should spend much more money than it takes in through taxes. By pumping more money into the economy, the government would stimulate more spending by both consumers and business and get the economy moving again.

*[Continued on next page.]*

*[Continued from previous page.]*

_____ 7. What the country should do is adopt a "share the wealth" program. The government should confiscate (take away) all the wealth of people who have more than $50,000 and share it with the poor who are suffering.

_____ 8. The government should expand the military and start a huge arms build up. All the people will then be employed. People will feel they are contributing to the strength of the nation, and businessmen and government would be cooperating to get the country out of the Depression. People should be made to think of what is good for our nation, and not themselves.

_____ 9. The workers must take over all the industries in the country. The government, controlled by the common people, should abolish (do away with) private ownership of businesses and take them over for the people. Workers would no longer be exploited by the businessmen and would be truly free. Only in this way can the country get out of the Depression and avoid future depressions.

_____ 10. Private charities should help the poor to survive. The government really has no legitimate role in aiding the poor. Government welfare causes people to lose incentive to work—it destroys the moral fiber of the country.

## The Political Spectrum

What does it mean when a person says that Senator Smith is a liberal, or that Congressman Jones is a conservative? The terms "liberal" and "conservative" are very complex, and different people give them different meanings. The characteristics which follow will help you better understand the way people commonly use these terms today regarding domestic issues (not foreign policy).

| Liberals tend to: | Conservatives tend to : |
|---|---|
| Turn to the government to solve economic problems. | Turn to business and the market to solve economic problems. |
| Favor government regulation of business. | Oppose government regulation of business. |
| Favor more equality over more freedom. | Favor more freedom over more equality. |
| Oppose larger defense budgets. | Support larger defense budgets. |
| Favor more government spending to solve economic problems. | Oppose more government spending. |
| Favor higher taxes on rich people. | Oppose higher taxes on rich people. |
| Favor political and economic change. | Oppose political and economic change. |

*[Continued on next page.]*

*[Continued from previous page.]*

The terms "liberal" and "conservative" can be put onto something called a political spectrum.

| A | B | C | D | E |
|---|---|---|---|---|
| RADICAL | LIBERAL | MODERATE | CONSERVATIVE | REACTIONARY |

"Radicals" (sometimes referred to as the left wing) tend to favor even more government intervention, more equality, and more extreme change than liberals. "Moderates" are between liberals and conservatives. "Reactionaries" (sometimes referred to as the right wing or radical right) tend not only to oppose change but also to want to go back to earlier times.

 Go back and label each of the ten proposals in this lesson with the letter corresponding to its position on the political spectrum. That is, if you feel a proposal is radical, you would put an "A" on the line next to the proposal, and so on.

# LESSON 16    Was the New Deal Good or Bad for the Country?

During the 1930's Depression, the administration of Franklin D. Roosevelt set up a program called the New Deal to help the country get back on its feet. Below are two viewpoints on whether the New Deal actually helped the country. Read them and answer the questions that follow.

## Historian A

The New Deal hurt our country a great deal. Our economy was in bad shape in 1932, but the New Deal only made matters worse in the long run. The Roosevelt Administration allowed intellectuals and socialists into the government, and these men used their positions to interfere with the normal functioning of the economy. There was too much experimentation—the New Deal confused action with progress.

One of the biggest problems created by the New Deal was an expanding bureaucracy. The federal government got much larger, which led to many of the problems we have today—waste, corruption, inefficiency, and high taxes. Our national debt rose from $19 billion in 1932 to $40 billion in 1939. People started thinking that America was a "Handout State" that could use unlimited spending to cure problems. The giveaway programs are continuing to ruin the moral fiber of America; people do not want to work when they are taken care of by the government.

The New Deal also created class jealousies. Businessmen felt that all kinds of regulations were put on them, while workers and farmers were pampered. They felt private enterprise was being strangled by creeping socialism.

One of the biggest criticisms of the New Deal, however, is that it did not do what it set out to do—it did not get the country out of the Depression. In 1938 the economy was still sick—with a low GNP and high unemployment. It remained for World War II to get us out of the Depression.

## Historian B

Franklin Roosevelt provided strong leadership in the 1930s when the country sorely needed it. No one really knows how far his New Deal got us out of the Depression because World War II came along and pulled us back to complete prosperity. We do know that the country was becoming more prosperous by 1936, but then a recession hit and we lost it all. To what extent the recession was a temporary setback in an otherwise general trend toward prosperity is a matter of opinion.

Even if the New Deal did not completely get the country out of the Depression, it must be remembered that its main goal was relief, not recovery. Under it, no one was allowed to starve—everyone kept his self-respect. The New Deal relieved the worst crisis of 1933 and saved the economy from collapse or revolution. Those businessmen who criticize the New Deal owe their livelihood partly to the efforts of Roosevelt.

The New Deal also achieved long-term reform of our economy. It changed our country's philosophy to one in which

[Continued on next page.]

## Historian B

*[Continued from previous page.]*

the government has a legitimate role to play in the economy to prevent mass hunger and injustice. In the process, the New Deal achieved a fairer distribution of national income and purged capitalism of some of its worst abuses.

 ## Historian A

1.  What is the main point of Historian A?

2.  In which sentence(s) (or none) is evidence offered to support Historian A's case?

3.  What assumption does Historian A make in the first paragraph, third sentence?

4.  In the second paragraph, third sentence, Historian A says, "Our national debt rose from $19 billion in 1932 to $40 billion in 1939," to support the argument that the New Deal brought about many problems. Evaluate the reasoning in this argument.

*[Continued on next page.]*

*[Continued from previous page.]*

 **Historian B**

5.  What is the main point of Historian B?

6.  In which sentence(s) (or none) is evidence offered to support Historian B's case?

7.  In the third sentence of the second paragraph, Historian B says the New Deal "saved the economy from collapse or revolution." What fallacy does this argument commit? (See pp. 8–16 in the "Guide to Critical Thinking" [Unit 1].)

8.  Evaluate the argument in the second sentence of the second paragraph. "Under it [the New Deal] no one was allowed to starve—everyone kept his self-respect."

*[Continued on next page.]*

*[Continued from previous page.]*

 **General Questions**

9.  Which argument is stronger? Why do you think so?

10. Under each cartoon write which viewpoint it would support.

Library of Congress Collection

Library of Congress Collection

A. Which viewpoint would it support? Why do you think so?

B. Which viewpoint would it support? Why do you think so?

## LESSON 17 Assessing the Reliability of Sources

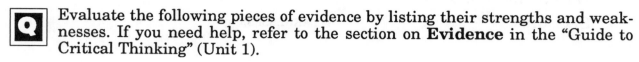 Evaluate the following pieces of evidence by listing their strengths and weaknesses. If you need help, refer to the section on **Evidence** in the "Guide to Critical Thinking" (Unit 1).

1. We are trying to determine whether the United States or the Soviet Union (U.S.S.R.) was responsible for starting the Cold War. We find the book *Speaking Frankly* (1947) by United States Secretary of State James F. Byrnes in which he describes his 1945 and 1946 negotiations with the Soviet leaders. Byrnes says the agreements were a success, but the Soviets soon violated (broke) the agreements, which started the Cold War.

   STRENGTHS:                          WEAKNESSES:

2. Secretary of State Dean Acheson responded in a February 3, 1949, State Department publication to the accusation that the United States (and especially the State Department) had been responsible for the Communist takeover of China. He said, "The unfortunate but inescapable fact is that the ominous result of the civil war in China was beyond the control of the government of the United States."

   STRENGTHS:                          WEAKNESSES:

3. We want to know if North Korea really did attack South Korea in June 1950. We find statements by the United Nations (UN) Security Council and General

*[Continued on next page.]*

*[Continued from previous page.]*

Assembly that North Korea attacked. The governments of South Korea and the United States also say North Korea attacked, as do newspapers from all countries except Communist countries. (Evaluate the strengths and weaknesses of the evidence from the UN.)

STRENGTHS:                           WEAKNESSES:

4. We want to know if the Soviets lied when they said they did not put missiles in Cuba. We find aerial photographs taken by United States reconnaissance planes showing the missile sites. We also find that the Soviets later took missiles out of Cuba. (Evaluate the aerial photographs.)

STRENGTHS:                           WEAKNESSES:

5. We want to know why the United States started the effort in 1947, known as the Marshall Plan, to rebuild the economies of Europe. We find a statement by George Marshall (author of the plan) in the *New York Times* of June 1947 explaining the reasons for the plan.

STRENGTHS:                           WEAKNESSES:

# LESSON 18    Identifying Assumptions and Analyzing Value Judgments

## Identify Unstated Assumptions

**Q** Identify the unstated assumptions in the following. If you need help, refer to the section on **Assumptions** in the "Guide to Critical Thinking" (Unit 1).

1. You should have me help you make decisions. Otherwise, if you make decisions on your own, you might make poor ones which I will have to straighten out or overrule.

2. Oh no! My science teacher wants to see me after school today.

3. (Statement in 1946) If the United States agrees to Soviet demands now, we will be faced with greater Soviet demands later.

4. Secretary of State George Marshall said that the United States should send economic aid to European countries because a healthier economy in Europe would prevent the spread of Communism.

5. In the late 1940s the United States should have sent troops into China to help the Nationalists defeat the Communists.

6. Secretary of State John Foster Dulles said in 1954 that the United States would rely on the threat of massive nuclear retaliation rather than American soldiers to stop Soviet or Chinese aggression (attacks) against free countries.

*[Continued on next page.]*

*[Continued from previous page.]*

## Value Judgments

 Some arguments contain value judgments. To evaluate value judgments, separate them from the factual part of the arguments, then think of cases where the value judgement would apply. See page 17 of the "Guide to Critical Thinking" (Unit 1) for more explanation on **Evaluating Value Statements**. The first one is done for you.

7. "The United States promised in the Yalta Agreement that Russia would get $10 billion in reparations [payment for damages] from Germany. Later the United States broke the Agreement. Thus, it was America that caused the disagreements about reparations."

    Conclusion: *America caused the disagreements about reparations.*

    Factual: *The United States promised $10 billion in reparations to Russia, then broke the agreement.*

    Value judgment: *Countries should keep their promises. You should always keep a promise.*

    Case where this value judgment might be wrong: *If the other country broke the agreement first, then the deal is off.*

8. "The U.S.S.R. promised to hold free elections in eastern Europe and then didn't hold them. This is one of the main causes of the Cold War."

    Conclusion:

    Factual:

    Value judgment:

    Case where this value judgment might be wrong:

9. "The U.S.S.R. didn't appreciate our lend-lease aid during World War II, so we were justified in cutting off the aid as soon as the war ended."

    Conclusion:

    Factual:

    Value judgment:

    Case where this value judgment might be wrong:

10. "The U.S.S.R. took over eastern Europe to prevent a possible future German attack. The Russians couldn't let Germany attack them again."

    Conclusion:

    Factual:

    Value judgment:

    Case where this value judgment might be wrong:

# LESSON 19    Identifying and Analyzing Types of Reasoning

## Identify and Evaluate the Types of Reasoning

 Identify and evaluate the type of reasoning used in each item below by asking and then answering the appropriate question(s). Read pp. 4–11 in the "Guide to Critical Thinking" (Unit 1) if you need more help. Remember, each item could contain more than one type of reasoning. Look for the reasoning that is most important.

---

The types of reasoning and key questions are:

**Cause and Effect** —Is there a reasonable connection between the cause and the effect?
* Are there other possible causes for this effect?
* Are there important previous causes that led to the proposed cause?

**Generalization**—How large and representative is the sample?

**Comparison**—How are the two cases similar and different?
* Do the similarities outweigh the differences?

---

1. We should have won the football game, but the officials made a bad call on a key fourth-down play. We lost our momentum after that and the other team rolled over us.

    Type of Reasoning:

    Evaluation:

2. If the Contras were to win a military victory and take over Nicaragua, it would in reality be a United States chosen puppet regime imposed on the Nicaraguan people by United States weapons and United States trained guerrillas. It would be the equivalent of what Moscow did in Eastern Europe (Poland, Hungary, etc.).

    Type of Reasoning:

    Evaluation:

*[Continued on next page.]*

---

*[Continued from previous page.]*

3.  A telephone poll of 612 adult Americans, taken by the Yankelovich, Clancy, Shulman Company on July 9, 1987, shows that at that time, 60% called themselves sympathetic to Oliver North, and 51% thought North was totally truthful in his testimony.

    Type of Reasoning:

    Evaluation:

4.  President Kennedy was wrong in taking strong action to get the Soviet missiles out of Cuba in 1962. The Soviet missiles in Cuba were no more of a threat to the United States than American missiles in Turkey were to Russia.

    Type of Reasoning:

    Evaluation:

5.  President Kennedy, after reading the book, *The Guns of August,* concluded that countries taking the hard line pushed each other into World War I. He decided not to take a hard line with the Soviet Union in the Cuban Missile Crisis lest he push the two countries into nuclear war.

    Type of Reasoning:

    Evaluation:

6.  After winning stunning victories in South Korea, United Nations forces invaded Communist North Korea. This led to a counter-invasion by a Chinese Communist army.

    Type of Reasoning:

    Evaluation:

*[Continued on next page.]*

*[Continued from previous page.]*

## Evaluate These Arguments

The arguments below cannot be evaluated according to the above questions, but something is wrong with them.

 What fallacy does the argument in 7 commit? See p. 6 and pp. 12–14 in the "Guide to Critical Thinking" (Unit 1) for the possible fallacies. What's wrong with the slide in 8?

7. "President Kennedy's decision to blockade Cuba in the 1962 Missile Crisis was brilliant. On the one hand, he avoided risking nuclear war by not choosing the dangerous option of bombing the missile sites. On the other hand, he did not back down to the Soviet threat, and thereby showed the Russians that they couldn't push us around." What fallacy does this argument commit?

8. In July 1987 Oliver North used the slide below to support the argument that Nicaragua (a Communist country) was a threat to Central America, so the United States should give more money to the Contras to oppose the Nicaraguan government. What's wrong with this slide?

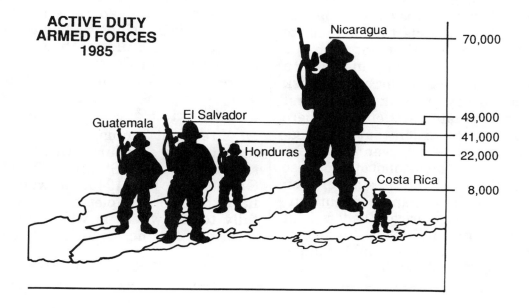

ACTIVE DUTY ARMED FORCES 1985

Nicaragua — 70,000
El Salvador — 49,000
Guatemala — 41,000
Honduras — 22,000
Costa Rica — 8,000

# LESSON 20

## Was the United States Justified in Dropping the Atomic Bombs on Japan?

## Background Information

For the United States, World War II began with a sneak attack by Japanese planes on American naval forces at Pearl Harbor. The war was fought in Europe against the Germans and their allies, and in the Pacific against the Japanese. During the war the secret Manhattan Project was commissioned to develop an atomic bomb for the United States. Germany surrendered (May 1945) before the bombs were completed, but on August 6, 1945, a single atomic bomb destroyed Hiroshima, and on the ninth, another atomic bomb destroyed Nagasaki.

In this lesson two viewpoints are presented on the controversial use of the atomic bombs. Read and evaluate them according to the criteria your teacher tells you. Consider the relevant information which follows the two viewpoints.

### Historian A

(1) Some historians argue that dropping the atomic bombs on Japan was justified because it shortened the war, thus saving lives in the end. This view is wrong. The United States was not justified in dropping the bombs.

(2) In the summer of 1945, the Japanese were almost totally defeated. American ships and planes pounded the island without any response by the Japanese. Leaders in Japan were trying to surrender and American leaders knew it. Several times the Japanese went to the Russians to ask them to mediate a peace settlement with the United States.[1] (It is not unusual for a country that wants to surrender to ask another country to speak for it at first and help negotiate a settlement.) There was only one condition that the Japanese insisted on—they wanted to keep their Emperor, the symbol of Japanese culture. The United States never even talked with the Japanese about surrender terms—American leaders kept demanding unconditional surrender. After we used the bombs and the Japanese surrendered, we let them keep their Emperor anyway. We could have allowed the Japanese to surrender earlier and saved all those lives obliterated by the bombs by letting them have their one condition in the first place.

(3) If the bombs were not used to bring about surrender, then why were they used? The plain truth is that they were used to scare Russia. In 1945 the United States disagreed with the Soviet Union in regard to Russia's actions in Europe. Our leaders felt that by showing the Russians we had a powerful weapon, we could get them to agree to our terms in Europe and Asia. As Secretary of War Stimson said in his diary, in diplomacy the bomb would be a "master card."[2]

(4) President Truman had an important meeting scheduled with the Russian leader, Josef Stalin, at Potsdam, Germany in July 1945. He wanted to have the bomb completed and successfully tested when he went into that meeting. Atomic scientist J. Robert

*[Continued on next page.]*

## Historian A

*[Continued from previous page.]*

Oppenheimer said, "We were under incredible pressure to get it [the bomb] done before the Potsdam meeting."[3] Truman hoped to have the bomb sticking out of his hip pocket, so to speak, when he negotiated with Stalin. Then he could make new demands of the Russians regarding eastern Europe. He told some of his friends at Potsdam before the final test, "If it explodes as I think it will, I'll certainly have a hammer on those boys."[4]

*(5)* While Truman was negotiating in Potsdam, the bomb was successfully tested in New Mexico, and he became more demanding with Stalin. Secretary of War Stimson stated, "He [Truman] said it [the bomb] gave him an entirely new feeling of confidence...."[5]

*(6)* But the Russians had to see the power of the bomb before the United States could intimidate them with it. This was accomplished at Hiroshima. Truman remarked, "This is the greatest thing in history!"[6]

*(7)* A second motive for dropping the bomb was to end the war in Asia before the Russians could get involved. The Japanese were talking of surrender, but the United States wanted surrender within days, not a negotiated surrender taking weeks to complete. The Russians had agreed at Yalta to enter the war against Japan three months after the end of the war in Europe. This would be three months after May 9, or somewhere around August 9. If the Russians got involved in the war in Asia, they could spread Communism to China and other countries and possibly to Japan itself. American leaders did not want to see this happen.[7]

*(8)* If the United States could speed up the Japanese surrender, we could avoid all these problems. We dropped the first bomb on August 6; Russia entered the war on the eighth, and we dropped the second bomb on the ninth. Don't these dates look suspicious? No country could surrender in only three days—it takes longer than that to make such an important decision. We would not wait longer because we wanted Japan to surrender before the Russians could get involved.

*(9)* Some scientists who worked on the bomb recommended that it not be dropped on people. They proposed that the United States demonstrate the bomb's power to Japanese leaders by dropping it on an uninhabited island. American political leaders rejected this idea. The devastating effect of the bomb had to be shown by destroying a city.

*(10)* Even top military leaders opposed the use of the atomic bomb.[8] The bomb would have little effect on the war, they argued, since the Japanese were already trying to surrender.

*(11)* All this evidence shows that the atomic bombs were not used to end the war and save lives, but rather to scare the Russians and speed up the end of the war before Russian influence spread further into Asia. The killing of over 100,000 civilians in one country in order to scare the leaders of another country was wrong. The United States was not justified in dropping the atomic bombs.

*[Continued on next page.]*

*[Continued from previous page.]*

## *Endnotes for Historian A* (All are quotes from the sources cited except bracketed portions.)

[1] Gar Alperovitz (a historian), *Atomic Diplomacy* (1965). (Direct quotations from *Foreign Relations Papers of the United States: Conference at Berlin,* Vol. II, pp. 1249, 1250, 1260, 1261.)

"On July 17, the day of the first plenary session, another intercepted Japanese message showed that although the government felt that the unconditional surrender formula involved too great a dishonor, it was convinced that 'the demands of the times' made Soviet mediation to terminate the war absolutely essential. Further cables indicated that the one condition the Japanese asked was preservation of 'our form of government.' A message of July 25 revealed instructions to the [Japanese] Ambassador in Moscow to go anywhere to meet with [Soviet Foreign Minister] Molotov during the recess of the Potsdam meeting so as to 'impress them with the sincerity of our desire' to terminate the war. He was told to make it clear that 'we should like to communicate to the other party [the United States] through appropriate channels that we have no objection to a peace based on the Atlantic Charter.' The only 'difficult point is the...formality of unconditional surrender.'"

James F. Byrnes (Secretary of State), *All in One Lifetime,* p. 297:

"July 28: Secretary Forrestal arrived and told me in detail of the intercepted messages from the Japanese government to Ambassador Sato in Moscow, indicating Japan's willingness to surrender."

[2] Stimson (Secretary of War) Diary , May 15:

"The trouble is that the President has now promised apparently to meet Stalin and Churchill on the first of July [at Potsdam] and at that time these questions will become burning and it may become necessary to have it out with Russia on her relations to Manchuria and Port Arthur and various other parts of North China, and also the relations of China to us. Over any such tangled web of problems the S-1 secret [the atomic bomb] would be dominant and yet we will not know until after...that meeting, whether this is a weapon in our hands or not. We think it will be shortly afterwards, but it seems a terrible thing to gamble with such big stakes in diplomacy without having your master card in your hand."

Leo Szilard (an atomic scientist who opposed use of the bombs on Japan), Conversation with Secretary of State Byrnes. Recorded on August 24, 1944, in Stewart to Bush, Atomic Energy Commission Document 200. Manhattan Engineering District—Top Secret, National Archives, Record Group 77, Box 7, folder 12; Box 14, folder 4:

[Szilard argued that we should not use the bomb.]

"Byrnes - Our possessing and demonstrating the bomb would make Russia more manageable in Europe."

"Szilard - [The] interests of peace might best be served and an arms race avoided by not using the bomb against Japan, keeping it secret, and letting the Russians think that our work on it had not succeeded."

"Byrnes - How would you get Congress to appropriate money for atomic energy research if you do not show results for the money which has been spent already?"

[3] Atomic Energy Commission, Oppenheimer Hearings, p. 31.

[4] Jonathan Daniels (biographer), *The Man of Independence* (1950), p. 266.

[5] *Foreign Relations Papers of the United States: Conference at Berlin,* 1945, Vol. II, p. 1361.

Stimson Diary, July 22:

"Churchill read Grove's report [on the successful testing of the atomic bomb in New Mexico] in full....He said, 'Now I know what happened to Truman yesterday. I couldn't understand it. When he got to the meeting after having read this report he was a changed man. He told the Russians just where they got on and off and generally bossed the whole meeting.'"

[6] Harry S. Truman, *Year of Decisions,* p. 421.

[7] Byrnes, *All in One Lifetime,* p. 300:

"Though there was an understanding that the Soviets would enter the war three months after Germany surrendered, the President and I hoped that Japan would surrender before then."

*[Continued on next page.]*

## *Endnotes for Historian A*
*[Continued from previous page.]*

Secretary of War Stimson stated in his diary on August 10, 1945, that he urged the President that:

"The thing to do was to get this surrender through as quickly as we can before Russia should get down in reach of the Japanese homeland....It was of great importance to get the homeland into our hands before the Russians could put in any substantial claim to occupy and help rule it."

[8] General Dwight Eisenhower, statement in "Ike on Ike," *Newsweek*, November 11, 1963, p. 107:

"I voiced to him [Secretary of War Stimson] my grave misgivings, first on the basis of my belief that Japan was already defeated and that dropping the bomb was completely unnecessary and secondly, because I thought our country should avoid shocking world opinion by the use of a weapon whose employment was, I thought, no longer necessary as a measure to save American lives. It was my belief that Japan was, at the very moment, seeking some way to surrender with a minimum loss of 'face.'...It wasn't necessary to hit them with that awful thing."

Admiral W.D. Leahy, *I Was There* (1950), p. 441:

"It was my opinion that the use of this barbarous weapon at Hiroshima and Nagasaki was of no material assistance in our war against Japan. The Japanese were already defeated and ready to surrender."

Air Force Chief of Staff LeMay, *New York Herald Tribune*, September 21, 1945:

"The atomic bomb had nothing to do with the end of the war."

---

## Historian B

*(1)* Dropping atomic bombs on Hiroshima and Nagasaki helped the United States avoid a costly invasion of Japan. It therefore saved lives in the long run, which makes it a justifiable action.

*(2)* It is true that the United States received some indication in the summer of 1945 that Japan was trying to surrender. Japan would not surrender unconditionally, however, and that was very important to the United States. The Germans had not surrendered unconditionally at the end of World War I and, as a result, they rose again to bring on World War II. The United States was not going to let that mistake happen again. As President Roosevelt said, "This time there will be no doubt about who defeated whom."[1]

*(3)* Although the Japanese military situation in July 1945 was approaching total defeat, many Japanese leaders hoped for one last ditch victory in order to get softer peace terms.[2] One of their hopes was to divide the Grand Alliance by getting Russia (which was not at the time at war with Japan) to be the intermediary for peace negotiations. Maybe the Allies would begin to disagree, the Japanese militarists reasoned, and Japan would get off easy. Their other hope was that they could inflict enough casualties on the American troops, or hold out long enough, to get the American public to pressure their leaders to accept something less than unconditional surrender.[3]

*(4)* Some historians argue that the only issue which prevented the Japanese from accepting unconditional surrender was their fear that the Emperor would be removed by the Americans. American leaders, however, believed that allowing this one condition would encourage the militarists in Japan to further resistance. Americans also felt that it would weaken the war effort in

*[Continued on next page.]*

---

## Historian B

*[Continued from previous page.]*

the United States since we would be deviating from our well-publicized policy of unconditional surrender.[4]

(5) Some Japanese leaders wanted much more, however, than just the one condition of keeping their Emperor. They wanted their troops to surrender to them, and they wanted no occupation of Japan or war crimes trials of Japanese leaders. Even on August 9, after the bombing of Hiroshima and Nagasaki, and after the Russian declaration of war against them, the Japanese leaders still could not agree to surrender.[5] This shows that the bombs were necessary—anything less than the bombs or invasion would not have brought about unconditional surrender.

(6) Some people believe that the dates of dropping the bombs (August 6 and 9) show that the United States dropped them to stop Russian entry into the war (August 8). There are two problems with this line of reasoning. First, the United States did not know the exact date of Russian entry. Second, the bombs were to be dropped when a military officer decided that the weather was right.[6] If Truman wanted to beat the Russians, why didn't he order the bombs to be dropped sooner, or why didn't he give in on unconditional surrender?

(7) The argument that the United States dropped the bombs in order to threaten the Russians is also weak. The fact that we were so unsuccessful in getting the Russians to agree to our policies in Europe shows that the bomb was not used for that reason. It must have been used to shorten the war. It certainly did not scare the Russians.

(8) Some American scientists opposed using the bomb on civilian or military targets, preferring to demonstrate it on an uninhabited island. This recommendation was studied carefully by a committee (the Interim Committee) set up to consider how to use the bomb. The committee said that a demonstration could have had a lot of problems, which would have wasted one of the bombs and precious time. In light of the fact that it took two bombs dropped on cities to bring about a surrender, the demonstration idea does not seem like it would have been effective. The committee recommended the bombs be used against military targets.[7]

(9) It is important to remember that on July 26, 1945, the United States warned the Japanese that we would use the atomic bomb against them unless they accepted unconditional surrender.[8] The fanatical Japanese leaders would not give in. They said they would ignore the warning.[9] Thus, the loss of life from the atomic bombings was the responsibility of the Japanese leaders, not the Americans.

(10) The United States was right in insisting on unconditional surrender. Since the Japanese would not surrender unconditionally, and since a demonstration bombing would not have been effective, the only alternative to using the atomic bombs was continuing the war. This would have cost hundreds of thousands more lives. In the long run, the use of the atomic bombs on Hiroshima and Nagasaki shortened the war and saved lives.

*[Continued on next page.]*

*[Continued from previous page.]*

## *Endnotes for Historian B* (All are quotes from the sources cited except bracketed portions.)

[1] President Roosevelt at a press conference, *F.D.R.: Public Papers of the Presidents*, Vol. XIII, p. 210:

> "Practically all Germans deny the fact they surrendered in the last war, but this time they are going to know it. And so are the Japs."

[2] *Command Decisions* (a history of World War II), p. 504, quotes a study done by Brigadier General George A. Lincoln, 4 June 1945:

> "In allied intelligence Japan was portrayed as a defeated nation whose military leaders were blind to defeat....Japan was still far from surrender. She had ample reserves of weapons and ammunition and an army of 5,000,000 troops, 2,000,000 of them in the home islands....In the opinion of the intelligence experts, neither blockade nor bombing alone would produce unconditional surrender before the date set for invasion [November 1945]. And the invasion itself, they believed, would be costly and possibly prolonged."

[3] *Command Decisions*, p. 517:

> "The militarists [in the Japanese Government] could and did minimize the effects of the bomb, but they could not evade the obvious consequences of Soviet intervention, which ended all hope of dividing their enemies and securing softer peace terms."

[4] *Command Decisions*, pp. 512–13, summarizing former Secretary of State Cordell Hull, *Memoirs*, Vol. II, p. 1593:

> "[Cordell] Hull's view...was the proposal [by Secretary of War Stimson to let the Japanese keep the Emperor] smacked of appeasement....The proposal to retain the imperial system might well encourage resistance [by the Japanese] and have 'terrible political repercussions' in the United States."

[5] Robert Butow (a historian), *Japan's Decision to Surrender* (1959), pp. 161, 163, 164. (Describing the debate among the six Japanese leaders about whether to surrender, August 9, 1945.)

> "While Susuki, [Prime Minister], Togo [Foreign Minister] and Yonai [Navy Minister] were committed in varying degrees to an outright acceptance [of the Potsdam Declaration demanding unconditional surrender] on the basis of the sole reservation that the Imperial house would be maintained, Anami [War Minister], Umezu [Army Chief of Staff], and Toyoda [Navy Chief of Staff], felt quite differently....What gagged these men—all true 'Samurai' bred in an uncompromising tradition—were the other points Yonai had mentioned. They wanted either to prevent a security occupation entirely or to exclude at least the metropolis of Tokyo....So far as war criminals were concerned, they felt it should be Japan and not the victorious enemy who must try such cases. In effect, they also wanted to accept the surrender of their own men....

> "From the standpoint of making postwar rationalizations and of 'opening up the future of the country' it was psychologically vital for the Japanese army and navy to make it appear as if they had voluntarily disbanded their military might in order to save the nation and the world at large from the continued ravages of war. If they could do this, they could very easily later plant an appealing suggestion to the effect that the imperial forces of Great Japan had not really suffered defeat at all. For this reason, too, a security occupation and war crimes trials conducted by Allied tribunals had to be avoided at all costs....

> "Togo pointedly asked whether Japan could win the war if a collapse of the type [of negotiations] occurred. To this the military heads could only reply that although they were not certain of ultimate victory, they were still capable of one more campaign—a 'decisive' battle in the homeland....The Council was deadlocked."

[6] Memorandum to Major General I.R. Groves from Brigadier General T.F. Farrell
Subject: Report on Overseas Operations—Atomic Bomb:
27 September 1945

> "After the Hiroshima strike we scheduled the second attack for 11 August [local time]. On learning that bad weather was predicted for that time, we reviewed the status of the assembly

*[Continued on next page.]*

## *Endnotes for Historian B*
*[Continued from previous page.]*

work for the Fat Man [the second atomic bomb], our uncompleted test program, and readiness of the planes and crews. It was determined that with an all-out effort, everything could be ready for takeoff on the early morning of 9 August [local time], provided our final test of the Fat Man proved satisfactory, which it did. The decision turned out to be fortunate in that several days of bad weather followed 9 August."

[7] Interim Committee report, June 1, 1945, from Harry S. Truman, *Year of Decisions*, p. 419:

"Recommend unanimously:

"1. The bomb should be used against Japan as soon as possible.

"2. It should be used against a military target surrounded by other buildings.

"3. It should be used without prior warning of the nature of the weapon."

[8] Proclamation for Unconditional Surrender, July 26, 1945. *Foreign Relations Papers of the United States: Potsdam Papers*, Vol. II, p. 1258:

"Section 13: We call upon the government of Japan to proclaim now the unconditional surrender of the Japanese armed forces, and to provide proper and adequate assurance of their good faith in such action. The alternative for Japan is prompt and utter destruction."

[9] *Foreign Relations Papers of the United States: Potsdam Papers*, Document 12518, July 28, 1945. Japanese Prime Minister Suzuki to reporters:

"I believe the Joint Proclamation [the Potsdam Proclamation—warning Japan to accept unconditional surrender] by the three countries is nothing but a rehash of the Cairo Declaration [which also called on Japan to surrender]. As for the [Japanese] Government, it does not find any important value in it, and there is no other recourse but to ignore it entirely and resolutely fight for the successful conclusion of the war."

*[Continued on next page.]*

*[Continued from previous page.]*

## Relevant Information

1.  Harry S. Truman, *Year of Decisions*, p. 421:

    "[When I was informed of the successful bombing of Hiroshima] I was greatly moved. I telephoned [Secretary of State] Byrnes aboard ship to give him the news and then said to the group of sailors around me, 'This is the greatest thing in history. It's time for us to get home.' I could not keep back my expectation that the Pacific war might now be brought to a speedy end."

2.  Henry L. Stimson, (Secretary of War in 1945), "The Decision to Use the Atomic Bomb," *Harper's* CLCIV, February, 1947, p. 101. Report of the Scientific Panel, June 16, 1945:

    "The opinions of our scientific colleagues on the initial use of these weapons are not unanimous: they range from the proposal of a purely technical demonstration to that of the military application best designed to induce surrender."

3.  Joseph Davies (United States Ambassador to the Soviet Union in 1945) Diary, July 28, 1945:

    "[Secretary of State Byrnes] was having a hard time with reparations [for the Soviets] but the details as to the success of the atomic bomb, which he had just received, gave him confidence that the Soviets would agree as to these difficulties. Byrnes' attitude that the atomic bomb assured ultimate success in negotiations disturbed me more than his description of its success amazed me. I told him that threat wouldn't work, and might do irreparable harm."

4.  Meeting at the White House, June 18, 1945. President Truman wrote down a point made by the Joint Chiefs on invading Japan:

    "In all, it had been estimated [by the Joint Chiefs] that it would require until the late fall of 1946 to bring Japan to her knees."

5.  Joseph Grew, (Acting Secretary of State, May 1945), *Turbulent Era*, Vol. II, (Boston, 1952):

    "In the light of available evidence I, myself, and others felt and still feel that if such a categorical statement about the dynasty [that the Japanese would be allowed to keep it] had been issued in May 1945 the surrender elements in the [Japanese] government might well have been afforded by such a statement a valid reason and the necessary strength to come to an early clear-cut decision [for surrender before the bombs were dropped]."

# Atomic Bomb — Values Survey

 Suppose you found the following information. Check whether you think each would justify or not justify the United States dropping the atomic bombs on Japan in August 1945. Remember that the statements are not necessarily true. The question is, "If this statement is true, would it have justified or not justified the dropping of the atomic bombs?" In August 1945 the United States was not getting along with our ally, Russia, which was a Communist country.

| SUPPOSE YOU FOUND THAT | JUSTIFIED | NOT JUSTIFIED |
|---|---|---|
| 1. The United States warned the Japanese to surrender or be wiped out by the bombs. | | |
| 2. The United States dropped the bombs to end the war quickly and save many lives in the long run. | | |
| 3. The United States dropped the bombs primarily to scare the Russians and make them give in to our demands in Europe. | | |
| 4. The Japanese leaders were trying to surrender and the American leaders knew it. | | |
| 5. Although the Japanese leaders were thinking about surrendering, they had a lot of conditions (limits) to the surrender which would allow them to say later that they had not really surrendered. | | |
| 6. The United States dropped the bombs to end the war before the Russians could attack Japan and Manchuria. Otherwise the Russians would have gained control of parts of Japan and China. | | |
| 7. The United States could have demonstrated the bomb to the Japanese leaders on an uninhabited island. | | |
| 8. The United States never tried to discuss surrendering with the Japanese leaders. | | |
| 9. The head United States military leaders in 1945 were opposed to dropping the atomic bombs on Japanese cities. | | |
| 10. The United States had spent a lot of time and money on the bombs and wanted to see how they worked. | | |
| 11. The United States dropped the bombs as revenge for the Japanese attack on Pearl Harbor. | | |

# LESSON 21    Who Primarily Caused the Cold War?

## Background Information

Since Russia became a Communist country (renamed the Soviet Union or U.S.S.R.) in 1917 there has been hostility between it and the United States. This hostility is due in large part to the vast differences in ideology (set of beliefs) between the two countries. The Soviet Union, as a Communist country, believes in the overthrow of capitalists in all countries to provide more equality and, ultimately, freedom for the working classes (called proletariat). The United States, as a capitalist country, believes in individual rights and private property and, as such, is appalled by Soviet violations of rights and confiscation (government take over) of people's property. Thus, the two countries have been suspicious, fearful, and hostile toward each other.

During World War II the United States and the Soviet Union cooperated enough as allies to defeat Nazi Germany. Near the end of the war the old suspicions and hostility returned as the contrary ideologies reemerged. The tensions increased greatly after the war, reaching a peak in the late 1940s. Much of the tension arose over Soviet domination (take over) of Eastern Europe.

Historians call this tension and diplomatic hostility (but lack of all-out war) after World War II, the Cold War. In many respects, the Cold War continued through the 1950s, 1960s, 1970s, and 1980s. The fear and tension continued to a greater or lesser extent through the whole time period. During the Cuban Missile Crisis (1962), for example, tensions were very great indeed, while during the period of detente in the 1970s tensions were not so strong.

In 1989 the Soviets loosened some of their control over eastern Europe. The Berlin Wall was taken down and in 1990 Germany was reunited. Most historians and political experts say that the Cold War ended in 1989.

The question we are going to deal with in this lesson is: "Which side, the United States or the Soviet Union, was primarily responsible for causing the Cold War at the end of World War II?" There are many other issues which could be explored on the topic of the Cold War, and some people feel the question of which side caused the Cold War is not that important. Nevertheless, many historians do think it is important and continue to debate it, and many interesting arguments have been made on the topic.

There were many issues in the 1940s which were important to the origins of the Cold War, such as: reparations (war payments) to the Soviet Union from Germany, the division of Germany into zones of occupation, and crises in Turkey and Iran. These other issues have been debated by historians. In this lesson, however, we will stick to issues revolving around eastern Europe, especially Soviet control of the region.

You will read two interpretations about how the Cold War began and who was responsible for it. Follow the instructions your teacher gives you.

*[Continued on next page.]*

*[Continued from previous page.]*

In order to understand the debate on the Cold War, you need to understand some terms used in the controversy.

**Revisionists** Historians who primarily blame the United States for starting the Cold War.

**Self-determination** The right of each country to rule itself free from outside interference.

**Spheres of influence** A strong country dominates weaker countries in an area. Spheres of influence conflict, at least to some extent, with self-determination since when a weak country is dominated by another country, it is not ruling itself free from outside interference.

**Traditionalists** Historians who believe that the Soviet Union was primarily responsible for the Cold War.

---

## Interpretation A

*(1)* Traditionalist historians believe that Soviet domination of eastern Europe was the main cause of the Cold War. A closer examination of what happened at the end of World War II reveals many weaknesses in this naively patriotic view. United States policy, not Soviet aggression, was the key to the problems between Russia and America.

*(2)* It is important to remember that the Soviet Union was invaded through eastern Europe by Germany during World War II. In this invasion millions of Soviets were killed. Josef Stalin, the Soviet leader, was committed to preventing any future invasions. He wanted governments in eastern Europe that would be friendly to the Soviet Union. Future aggressors would thereby have to attack these countries before reaching Soviet soil.

*(3)* Stalin believed in spheres of influence, and he thought he had an understanding with Prime Minister Churchill and President Roosevelt that eastern Europe was in the Soviet sphere of influence. After all, Britain had her own sphere of influence in the worldwide British Empire and the United States had its sphere of influence in Latin America. The United States telling Russia to give up its domination of Rumania would be like the Soviets telling the Americans to give up their domination of Mexico.

*(4)* Moreover, Stalin and Churchill had made an agreement in October 1944 to divide eastern Europe into spheres of influence: Rumania and Bulgaria were to be the "main concern" of the U.S.S.R., Greece was to be the "main concern" of Britain, and the two countries would have equal concern in Hungary and Yugoslavia.[1] When the United States approved the agreement on a trial basis,[2] Stalin must surely have felt that the three powers had reached an understanding that Europe was to be divided into spheres. Later, when the British smashed the Communists in Greece, Stalin did not help the Greek Communists, showing that he would abide by the agreement.[3]

*(5)* It was under these circumstances

*[Continued on next page.]*

## Interpretation A

*[Continued from previous page.]*

that the Russians moved into eastern Europe as they pushed back the Nazi invaders at the end of World War II. It is important to remember that most eastern European countries had never been democratic, and three of them (Rumania, Bulgaria, and Hungary) were allied with Germany during the war. Under the conditions of war, moreover, the Soviets sometimes had to take harsh measures in the areas they captured.

*(6)* Nevertheless, the Soviets did allow considerable freedom in eastern Europe. Free elections were held in several countries. Bulgaria's elections under Soviet occupation were declared to be the freest in the country's history.[4] Many Communists were elected throughout eastern Europe since Communists were popular, especially with poor peasants. Communists were popular because they had been underground fighters against the Germans and because they believed in dividing the wealthy landowners' property among the peasants.[5]

*(7)* One country in eastern Europe presented special problems for the Soviets—Poland. The Poles had a government in exile in London, England during the war. (Poland had been conquered by Germany in 1939.) The London Poles were hostile to Russia even before the Yalta Conference (where issues relating to Poland were negotiated). Poland demanded that they keep some Russian territory captured in 1920. Even Churchill agreed with the Russian claim to the land.[6] And the Polish underground threatened to fight the Russians (which would help the Germans) if the Russians moved into Poland before agreeing that the Poles would get the disputed land.[7]

*(8)* At Yalta in February 1945, Stalin insisted that the Lublin Poles (Polish Communist leaders who were pro-Soviet) control the new Polish government. He compromised and allowed the London Poles to have six of the twenty ministries in the new government. President Roosevelt himself said that the Lublin Poles were the basis of the new government according to the Yalta Agreements.[8]

*(9)* Stalin even agreed in the Declaration of Liberated Europe to the idea of free elections in eastern Europe. He knew that Roosevelt was interested, however, primarily in the *promise* of free elections. Roosevelt had told Stalin in 1943 at the Teheran Conference that he would not oppose Stalin's dominance over eastern Europe as long as it did not upset the millions of American voters of eastern-European background. He told the Soviet leader that the promise of an election would make Soviet dominance more acceptable to the American public.[9] The Declaration of Liberated Europe only called for the three powers—Britain, America, and Russia—to consult each other about starting self-governments. No country was obligated to do anything specific.[10] Stalin realized that the Declaration of Liberated Europe and the Agreement on Poland were negotiated by the Americans primarily to please the voters at home.

*(10)* Thus, the United States, Britain, and the Soviet Union had reached a series of agreements and understandings about the Soviet sphere of influence in eastern Europe up to April 1945. Within their sphere, the Soviets showed flexibility. In some countries there was considerable freedom and elections were held. All countries had to meet with Stalin's one overriding require-

*[Continued on next page.]*

## Interpretation A

*[Continued from previous page.]*

ment, however; they all had to be friendly to the Soviet Union.

*(11)* Then Roosevelt died and all the agreements and understandings fell apart. Harry Truman became President and, backed by the atomic bomb, he soon began attacking the Soviet sphere in eastern Europe. He said the Lublin Poles should not control most of the ministries in the Polish Government. He said the Russians could "go to hell."[11] The United States threatened the Soviets and began building up Germany again—the very thing the Russians feared most!

*(12)* The Russians began to tighten their grip on eastern Europe in response to these American threats, al-though in 1945 and 1946 they still allowed considerable freedom in Hungary, Bulgaria, Austria, and Czechoslovakia. Then in 1947, President Truman declared Cold War on the Soviet Union. In the Truman Doctrine he characterized the world as being divided into good (the United States) and evil (the Soviet Union). He said the Soviets relied on terror and oppression, and he said it was the policy of the United States to help other countries stop the Soviets.[12] The Russians now clamped down on eastern Europe to protect themselves. The Cold War had begun due to the hostile and uncompromising policies adopted by the Truman Administration.

## *Endnotes for Interpretation A*

[1] Winston Churchill, *Triumph and Tragedy* (1953), p. 227.

Meeting in Moscow, October 9, 1944:

"While this was being translated I wrote out on a half-sheet of paper:

Rumania
     Russia  90%
     The others  10%
Greece
     Great Britain (in accord with U.S.A.)   90%
     Russia  10%
Yugoslavia  50-50%
Hungary    50-50%
Bulgaria
     Russia  75%
     The others  25%

"I pushed this across to Stalin, who had by then heard the translation. There was a slight pause. Then he took his blue pencil and made a large tick upon it, and passed it back to us. It was all settled in no more time than it takes to set down."

[2] Briefing Book enclosed in a letter, January 24, 1945, *Foreign Relations Papers of the United States 1945, Conferences at Malta and Yalta* (hereafter *Yalta Papers*), pp. 104–5:

"AMERICAN POLICY TOWARD SPHERES OF INFLUENCE

"—Mr. Churchill suggested to the President [Roosevelt] that the arrangement [made between Churchill and Stalin on spheres of influence] be given a three-month's trial, subject then to review by the three Governments, to which the President's assent was given."

[3] Churchill, *Triumph and Tragedy*, p. 293:

"Stalin, however, adhered strictly and faithfully to our agreement of October, and during all

*[Continued on next page.]*

## Endnotes for Interpretation A
*[Continued from previous page.]*

the long weeks of fighting the Communists in the streets of Athens [Greece], not one word of reproach [criticism] came from *Pravda* or *Isvestia* [Soviet newspapers]."

[4] *Foreign Relations Papers of the United States* (hereafter *Foreign Relations*), 1945, Vol. II, p. 731:

"[Soviet Foreign Minister Molotov] read a press report taken from the *New York Times* concerning the orderly fashion in which the elections in Bulgaria had taken place. He said no one could deny the fact that there was wider participation in these elections than in any other in the history of Bulgaria."

[5] Zbigniew Brzezinski (historian, political scientist), *The Soviet Bloc* (1960), pp. 7, 19:

"To the peasants [of Eastern Europe] prospects of land reform held out a vision of the fulfillment of their most cherished dream, and one much too long denied.

"To most people in war-devastated Eastern Europe, rapid economic reconstruction was the most vital issue, even more so than politics. And to a majority of them, state planning [Communism] appeared necessary and logical.

"The rapid growth of its membership soon made the Communist Party the leading party [in Czechoslovakia]. It justified its claim to this distinction by polling 38 percent of the vote in the free elections held in April 1946."

Also, Martin Herz [historian], *Beginnings of the Cold War* (1966), pp. 135–36:

"Surprisingly free elections took place in Hungary under Soviet occupation in November 1945, in which the Smallholders [a conservative noncommunist party] obtained a smashing majority."

[6] Winston Churchill, *The Hinge of Fate* (1950), p. 327.

Churchill to President Roosevelt, April 23, 1942:

"The principles of the Atlantic Charter ought not to be construed so as to deny Russia the frontiers she occupied when Germany attacked her [which included the part of Poland that Russia was claiming]. This was the basis on which Russia acceded [agreed] to the Charter."

[7] Cordell Hull (American Secretary of State), *Memoirs*, Vol. II, p. 1316.

(Secretary Hull is describing a memorandum sent to him from the Polish Ambassador to the United States. The portion quoted is from the memorandum itself.)

"The Polish ambassador threatened that, if Soviet troops entered Polish territory without previous resumption of Polish-Soviet relations, the Polish Government would 'undertake political action against this violation of Polish sovereignty.'"

[8] *Foreign Relations, 1945*, Vol V., pp. 353–54.

The United States Ambassador in the Soviet Union (Averell Harriman) to the Secretary of State, Moscow, June 21, 1945–Midnight:

"Thus there will be six new Ministries out of a total of twenty....The fundamental basis of the reorganized government is that the Workers Party [Lublin], the Peasant Party [London] and the Socialist Party [Lublin] shall each have six portfolios and two are to be held by other democratic parties."

Also, Herbert Feis (historian), *Churchill, Roosevelt, Stalin—The War They Waged and the Peace They Sought* (1957), p. 575. (Note: The actual message was not published in 1957. Feis had access to official United States sources and quoted from the original document.)

Message to Churchill from Roosevelt:

"If we attempt to evade the fact that we placed, as clearly shown by the [Yalta] agreement, somewhat more emphasis on the Lublin Poles than on the other two groups from which the Government is to be drawn, we expose ourselves to the charge that we are attempting to go back on the Crimea [Yalta] decision."

[9] *Foreign Relations, 1943*, Vol. III, *The Teheran Conference*, pp. 594–95:

Roosevelt-Stalin Meeting, December 1, 1943, 3:20 p.m., Roosevelt's Quarters, Soviet Embassy

*[Continued on next page.]*

## Endnotes for Interpretation A
*[Continued from previous page.]*

(President Roosevelt is speaking to Marshal Stalin):

"He [Roosevelt] added that there were in the United States from six to seven million Americans of Polish extraction and, as a practical man, he did not wish to lose their vote.

"The President went on to say that there were a number of persons of Lithuanian, Latvian, and Estonian origin, in that order, in the United States.

"The President [said] it would be helpful for him personally if some public declaration in regard to the future elections, to which the Marshal [Stalin] had referred, could be made."

[10] Quoted in Martin Hertz, *Beginnings*, pp. ix–x.

Declaration on Liberated Europe, February 11, 1945:

"To foster the conditions in which the liberated peoples may exercise these rights [for self-government], the three governments will jointly assist the people....
(c) to form interim governmental authorities broadly representative of all democratic elements in the population and pledged to the earliest possible establishment through free elections of governments responsive to the will of the people; and (d) to facilitate where necessary the holding of such elections....

"When, in the opinion of the three governments, conditions in any European liberated state or any former Axis satellite state in Europe make such action necessary, they will immediately consult together on the measures necessary to discharge the joint responsibilities set forth in this declaration..."

Signed at Yalta by Prime Minister Churchill, President Roosevelt, and Premier Stalin.

[11] *Stalin Correspondence* (1951), Vol. II, pp. 218–19. (A collection of writings to and from Marshal Stalin during World War II, published by the Soviet Government. This particular excerpt is from a note from Truman to Stalin.)

"The United States Government cannot be a party to any method of consultation with Polish leaders which would not result in the establishment of a new Provisional Government of National Unity genuinely representative of the democratic elements of the Polish people."

Also, *Foreign Relations, 1945*, Vol. V, p. 253 (Truman speaking):

"Our agreements with the Soviet Union so far...[have] been a one-way street....If the Russians do not wish to join us, they could go to hell."

[12] Truman Doctrine, Speech before Congress, March 12, 1947. Quoted in John Lewis Gaddis, *The United States and the Origins of the Cold War*, p. 351:

"At the present moment in world history nearly every nation must choose between alternative ways of life. The choice is too often not a free one.

"One way of life is based upon the will of the majority, and is distinguished by free institutions, representative government, free elections, guarantees of individual liberty, freedom of speech and religion, and freedom from political oppression.

"The second way of life is based upon the will of a minority forcibly imposed upon the majority. It relies upon terror and oppression, a controlled press and radio, fixed elections, and the suppression of personal freedoms.

"I believe that it must be the policy of the United States to support free people who are resisting attempted subjugation by armed minorities or by outside pressures."

*[Continued on next page.]*

*[Continued from previous page.]*

## Interpretation B

*(1)* The Soviet takeover of eastern Europe after World War II was a major cause of the Cold War. Many of the disputes between the United States and the U.S.S.R. arose because of Soviet domination of this area. Amazingly, however, revisionist historians (such as Interpretation A) make excuses for the Soviet takeover and blame the resulting problems instead on the United States! The Russians, so the argument goes, had legitimate reasons for occupying eastern Europe—they wanted a buffer against future German attacks; they felt that the United States and Britain had spheres of influence of their own, so the U.S.S.R. was entitled to its sphere in eastern Europe; and they felt that their sphere in eastern Europe had been agreed to by the United States and Britain. This view is a serious distortion of the truth.

*(2)* While the Russians may have been concerned about future German attacks through eastern Europe, this was not an immediate worry since Germany was so weak after World War II. As will be shown, the Soviets gave this reason as an excuse to cover for the real reason for their takeover: the Russians actually took eastern Europe to spread Communism.

*(3)* The Soviets justified their control over eastern Europe on the basis of spheres of influence. They argued that the western Allies (Britain and America) had agreed that eastern Europe was in the Soviet sphere. This argument is based upon a 1944 agreement between Churchill and Stalin in which Britain was to have controlling interest in Greece; Russia was to have controlling interest in Rumania and Bulgaria; and the two countries were to have equal say in Yugoslavia and Hungary. In reality, however, Churchill made it clear that he meant "controlling interest" to apply only to wartime occupation and not to any postwar sphere of influence.[1] Moreover, the United States never consented to this agreement on a permanent basis. American leaders, taking a lesson from history, were consistently opposed to anything remotely close to sphere-of-influence arrangements made in secret.[2] They noticed what had happened when the European Allies made secret deals (in which the powers divided up territory among themselves) during World War I. When the arrangements were discovered and publicized, the prestige of the Allies had plummeted.

*(4)* Neither the British nor the Americans gave their consent to a Russian sphere of influence in eastern Europe after World War II. The fact that Russia also included Czechoslovakia and Poland in its area of domination, despite the fact that those two countries were not included in the Churchill-Stalin deal, leads one to the obvious conclusion that Russia would have taken eastern Europe no matter what the United States or Britain did anywhere—Greece, Italy, Belgium, Latin America, Japan, or anywhere else.[3]

*(5)* What is relevant to the Soviet takeover of eastern Europe is the Soviet signature, at the Yalta Conference, to the Declaration of Liberated Europe. In it the Soviets promised to establish representative governments based on free elections in the areas they liberated from the Nazis.[4] The fact that they did not carry out this promise is the most important issue regarding eastern Europe and puts the blame squarely with the U.S.S.R.[5]

*[Continued on next page.]*

## Interpretation B

*[Continued from previous page.]*

*(6)* The fate of Poland is one of the most tragic of the countries in eastern Europe after World War II. The developments in Poland symbolized the overall harsh Russian measures in eastern Europe.

*(7)* The Polish people, as well as the Polish government-in-exile in London, feared the consequences of the Russian army's advance in 1944 and 1945 as the Germans retreated. The cynical Nazi-Soviet Pact of 1939, in which Poland was divided between Germany and Russia, the Russian murder of 15,000 Polish officers in the Katyn Woods,[6] and the Russian refusal to help the Polish underground in Warsaw as it was being wiped out by the Germans[7] all showed the Poles that they had little reason to trust and much reason to fear Russia.

*(8)* As Russia "liberated" Poland, it became more and more obvious that the worst Polish fears would come true—Polish freedom was to be snuffed out. First, the Russians demanded that part of Poland be given to the U.S.S.R. This was in direct violation of the right of self-determination as set forth in the Atlantic Charter. The Russians, however, cared little for the rights of other countries. They next installed their own handpicked Communist government in Poland. This puppet government's leaders were trained in the town of Lublin in the U.S.S.R.[8] The United States protested at the Yalta Conference against rule by the Lublin Poles alone and, as a result, the Soviets promised to reorganize the Lublin Government on a broader democratic basis to include the London (pro-democracy) Poles, and to hold free elections.[9] The free elections were never held, and the Lublin Poles continued to rule the country, converting it into a Communist nation.[10] Russia thought little of Poland's right to self-determination.

*(9)* The Russians extinguished rights in a similar harsh fashion in all the eastern European countries.[11] The Soviet Union exercised totalitarian (total) control over the area (for example, they did not allow free speech) to the same extent that Hitler's Germany had controlled the countries it conquered. It is this type of domination which makes Russia's "sphere of influence" so different from the spheres of influence of other powers. It is true that Britain has more say about actions and policies in the countries in the British Empire than do other powers, and that the United States has more say about what goes on in Latin America than do other powers. The United States and Britain, however, do not dominate the countries in their respective spheres in the same way that Russia dominates the countries in her sphere. It is one thing for a country to be dominant in a smaller country's economy; it is quite another matter to take away all rights and freedoms in that smaller country.

*(10)* The reaction of the United States to Russian expansion into and domination of eastern Europe was entirely to be expected. The United States could not sit idly by while people had their freedom taken away. Thousands of Americans had died in World War II to preserve the freedom of countries threatened by aggressor nations. How could the United States now allow Soviet aggression in eastern Europe? American leaders realized that to "appease" a dictator (as Neville Chamberlain had done with Hitler at Munich when he allowed Hitler to take over

*[Continued on next page.]*

## Interpretation B

*[Continued from previous page.]*

part of Czechoslovakia in the hope that Hitler would demand no more territory) was to encourage further aggression.[12] If the United States conceded eastern Europe to Soviet control, then Stalin would soon be making attempts to control western Europe.[13] The peoples of both eastern and western Europe deserved the right to be left to choose their own leaders and their own types of government without interference from Communist Russia. In standing up for the rights of those people, the United States chose the only morally right course.

### *Endnotes for Interpretation B*

[1] Churchill, *Triumph and Tragedy*, October 12, 1944, pp. 233–34:

"The system of percentages [made in the meeting with Stalin; see endnote 1, Interpretation A] is not intended to prescribe the numbers sitting on commissions for the different Balkan countries, but rather to express the interest and sentiment with which the British and Soviet Governments approach the problems of these countries, and so that they might reveal their minds to each other in some way that could be comprehended. It is not intended to be more than a guide, and of course in no way commits the United States, nor does it attempt to set up a rigid system of spheres of interest. It may however help the United States to see how their two principal Allies feel about these regions when the picture is presented as a whole."

[2] Briefing Book enclosed in a letter, January 24, 1945, *Yalta Papers*, pp. 104–5.

American note sent to the Soviets and British about the October 9, 1944, agreement on percentages in eastern Europe:

"Our assent to the trial period of three months was given in consideration of the present war strategy. Except for this overriding consideration, this Government would wish to make known its apprehension lest the proposed agreement might, by the natural tendency of such arrangements, lead to the division in fact of the Balkan region into spheres of influence."

[3] *Foreign Relations*, 1945, Vol. V, pp. 232–33:

(Conversation between the President, the Secretary of State, and others)

April 20, 1945

"At the President's request, [American] Ambassador [to the Soviet Union, Averell] Harriman then made a brief report on his opinion of the present problems facing the United States in relation to the Soviet Union. He said that he thought the Soviet Union had two policies which they thought they could successfully pursue at the same time—one, the policy of cooperation with the United States and Great Britain, and the other, the extension of Soviet control over neighboring states through unilateral action. He said that he thought our generosity and desire to cooperate was being misinterpreted in Moscow by certain elements around Stalin as an indication that the Soviet Government could do anything that it wished without having trouble with the United States.

"Ambassador Harriman said that in effect what we were faced with was a "barbarian invasion of Europe," that Soviet control over any foreign country did not mean merely influence on their foreign relations, but the extension of the Soviet system with secret police, extinction of freedom of speech, etc., and that we had to decide what should be our attitude in the face of these unpleasant facts."

[4] For the text of the Declaration, see endnote 10, Interpretation A.

[5] James F. Byrnes, *Speaking Frankly* (1947), p. 52:

(The Soviet Ambassador to Rumania, Mr. Vyshinski, is arguing with the King of Rumania about

*[Continued on next page.]*

## Endnotes for Interpretation B
*[Continued from previous page.]*

appointing a new leader in the country.)

"Shortly afterward Mr. Vyshinski sent word to the King that the Communist leader, Petru Groza, was the choice of the Soviet Government.

"Mr. Vyshinski was quoted as saying that unless the King accepted the Groza government by the afternoon of the following day, he [Vyshinski] would not be responsible for the continuance of Rumania as an independent state."

Also, Truman Briefing Book for the Conference at Potsdam of July 1945, *Potsdam Papers*, Vol. I, pp. 258–59:

"The Russians have rejected British and American proposals that discussions should take place regarding the political situation in Rumania and elections in Bulgaria. These actions are not in accordance with the Crimea [Yalta] Declaration on Liberated Europe whereby the Big Three were to concert their policies in assisting the liberated peoples to solve their pressing political and economic problems by democratic means. Eastern Europe is, in fact, a Soviet sphere of influence."

[6] Herz (historian), *Beginnings of the Cold War* (1966), p. 45:

According to information available to the London Polish government, Lavrenty Beria, the head of the Soviet secret police, had declared to some Polish representatives as early as the spring of 1940 that in regard to the missing [Polish] officers, "a great mistake had been made."

On April 13, 1943, the German radio announced that on the basis of information furnished by the local population, the German authorities had found in the Forest of Katyn, near Smolensk, "the spot where in secret mass executions, the Bolsheviks [Russians] murdered 10,000 Polish officers."

[7] The Polish resistance fighters rose up in rebellion in Warsaw against the Germans as the Soviet Army approached the city, but the Russian army stopped while the Germans wiped out the Polish resistance.

Herz, *Beginnings of the Cold War*, p. 57:

"The Polish underground in Warsaw was soon opposed by five picked German divisions and it was clear that the fate of the uprising depended on the speed of the Russian advance into the city. The Russian troops, however, arranged themselves on the eastern bank of the Vistula to the north and south of Warsaw and marked time."

[8] Truman, *Year of Decisions*, p. 36:

"The tragic fact was that, though we were allies of Russia, we had not been permitted to send our observers into Poland. Russia was in full military occupation of the country at the time and had given her full support to the so-called Lublin government—a puppet regime of Russia's own making."

[9] Quoted in Herz, *Beginnings of the Cold War*, p. x.

Declaration on Poland, February 11, 1945:

"A new situation has been created in Poland as a result of her complete liberation by the Red Army. This called for the establishment of a Polish Provisional Government which can be more broadly based than was possible before the recent liberation of western Poland. The Provisional Government which is now functioning in Poland should therefore be reorganized on a broader democratic basis with the inclusion of democratic leaders from Poland itself and from Poles abroad. This new Government should then be called the Polish Provisional Government of National Unity....

"This Polish Provisional Government of National Unity shall be pledged to the holding of free and unfettered elections as soon as possible on the basis of universal suffrage and secret ballot. In these elections all democratic and anti-Nazi parties shall have the right to take part and to put forward candidates...."

Signed at Yalta by Prime Minister Churchill,

President Roosevelt, and Marshal Stalin

*[Continued on next page.]*

## Endnotes for Interpretation B
*[Continued from previous page.]*

[10] *Stalin Correspondence*, Vol. II, pp. 202–3.

Note to Stalin from Roosevelt, April, 1945:

"While it is true that the Lublin Government is to be reorganized and its members play a prominent role, it is to be done in such a fashion as to bring into being a new government. This point is clearly brought out in several places in the text of the Agreement. I must make it quite plain to you that any such solution which would result in a thinly disguised continuance of the present Warsaw regime [the Lublin Government] would be unacceptable and would cause the people of the United States to regard the Yalta agreements as having failed."

[11] "Study of Communism in Europe by the Special Assistant to the Director of European Affairs," enclosure in "Memorandum to the President, June 27, 1945," *Foreign Relations: Potsdam*, 1945, Vol. I, pp. 267–73.

(The study was completed on June 2, 1945.)

"The generally belligerent treatment of democratic forces by communist elements in all eastern European countries is well-known in spite of the strict news censorship imposed in those areas by the Russians and their satellites. Professing to applaud democratic practices, those Communists in power in eastern Europe have applied terror, intimidation, mass deportation and murder under the guise of necessary purges, all of which has proved shocking to our concept of democracy and free speech. It is plain that democracy to a Communist has not the same connotation it has to an occidental [European or American] democrat."

[12] See, for example, the opinion of Ambassador Harriman in endnote 3, above.

[13] "Study of Communism," in *Foreign Relations: Potsdam*, pp. 267–73.

"Within the past three months the Communist parties of France and Italy have openly advocated a return to fundamental Marxist-Leninist-Stalinist tactics. They declare that the time has come for a more radical solution of the economic and political conditions confronting those countries. The emphasis is again on the class character of the problem with the recommended solution lying in the expropriation of means of production [take-over of factories by the workers] and attacks on the capitalist class generally."

## Relevant Information

1. *Foreign Relations*, 1945, Volume V, pp. 252–255.

   Memorandum by Mr. Charles E. Bohlen, Assistant to the Secretary of State, of a Meeting at the White House, April 23, 1945, 2 p.m.:

   "The Secretary of State told the meeting that Mr. Molotov had arrived in good spirits yesterday and had had a good talk with the President yesterday evening but that at the Foreign Ministers meeting later great difficulties had developed over the Polish question. The continuance of the meeting this morning had produced no improvement and a complete deadlock had been reached on the subject of the carrying out of the Yalta agreement on Poland. The Secretary said that the truth of the matter was the Lublin or Warsaw Government was not representative of the Polish people and that it was now clear that the Soviet Government intended to try to enforce upon the United States and British Governments this puppet government of Poland and obtain its acceptance as the legal government of Poland.

   "The President said that he had told Mr. Molotov last night that he intended

*[Continued on next page.]*

## Relevant Information

*[Continued from previous page.]*

fully to carry out all the agreements reached by President Roosevelt at the Crimea [Yalta]. He added that he felt our agreements with the Soviet Union so far had been a one-way street and that could not continue; it was now or never. He intended to go on with the plans for San Francisco [for the United Nations] and if the Russians did not wish to join us they could go to hell. The President then asked in rotation the officials present for their view."

2. Stanislow Mikolajczyk, (Prime Minister of the Polish Government in London during World War II), *The Rape of Poland—Pattern of Soviet Aggression* (1948) p. 267:

   "Memorandum to the British Government—The Polish Government has, moreover, reasons to fear that in present conditions the life and property of Polish citizens may be exposed to danger after the entry of Soviet troops into Poland and the imposing on the country of Soviet administration. In that case, desperate reaction of the Polish community may be expected."

3. Zbigniew Brzezinski, *Soviet Bloc*, p. 12. Summarized from Mikolajczyk, *The Rape of Poland*:

   "In a free election he [Mikolajczyk] most certainly would have won a sweeping victory....But free elections were not likely to occur. In Poland of 1945, all the levers of power were in Communists' hands, the Red Army was on the scene, and the NKVD [secret police] was active. Mikolajczyk's popularity under these conditions had no political significance, while the growing awareness of the absence of effective Western support made it possible [for the Communists] to apply increasing doses of terror against the Polish Peasant Party. In 1947, after the manipulated elections formalized the liquidation of his party, Mikolajczyk escaped abroad."

4. March 6, 1946, *Foreign Relations: 1946*, Volume V, p. 516:

   George Kennan, Charge d'affairs to the U.S.S.R. (Diplomatic representative in charge of the embassy during the absence of the Ambassador):

   "There could be no doubt that Maurice Thorez, leader of the French Communist Party, was acting 'as [a] Moscow stooge.'"

5. Martin Herz, *Beginnings of the Cold War*, p. 136:

   "May 1945 Communists held 7 out of 25 Cabinet posts. Benes returned from London to rule Czechoslovakia in April 1945. Free elections were held in Czechoslovakia in 1946. Absolute control didn't come until 1948.

   "Czechoslovakia had a tradition of friendliness and cultural affinity with Russia...[which] was paralleled to some extent in Bulgaria and Yugoslavia."

# LESSON 22

## Was the United States Right to Get Involved in the Vietnam War?

## Background Information

The Vietnam War has a long history. In the 1880s the French established the colony of Indochina (Vietnam, Cambodia, and Laos) and ruled it until World War II, when the Japanese invaded and took over. In 1945 the Japanese were defeated and the French returned. A revolutionary group, the Vietminh, led by Ho Chi Minh, opposed the French, resulting in war from 1946 to 1954. The French left after their military defeat at Dien Bien Phu. Vietnam was split into North (led by Ho Chi Minh) and South (led by Ngo Dinh Diem). Fighting now broke out in South Vietnam between what was called the National Liberation Front (the NLF or Vietcong) and the South Vietnamese government. The NLF was backed by North Vietnam, Russia and China, while the United States supported the South Vietnamese government.

The United States sent advisers to South Vietnam in the early 1960s, and large numbers of American soldiers in 1965. The American phase of the war lasted until 1973, when the last United States troops were withdrawn. The war ended in 1975 with North Vietnam taking over all of South Vietnam and making it Communist.

Historians of the Vietnam War can be divided into two broad schools (groups) of thought. One says we should never have been involved in Vietnam and realistically we could not have won. The other says we were right to be involved and we should have persevered to win the war. These two points of view are represented in this lesson. As you read them, you will learn a lot more details about the war. After you have read them, answer the questions on the two interpretations.

Note: Viet Nam (two words) is more correct than Vietnam (one word), but most Americans write it as one word. The two word form has been preserved in book titles and quotes in this lesson, when the original source used it.

## Interpretation A

(1) The Vietnam War is a chapter of American history which many Americans would like to forget. The tragedy is that American involvement could have been avoided from the beginning. But American leaders, driven by fear of Communist expansion, committed ever increasing numbers of American men and amounts of American resources to a war which really was not in the country's national interest.

(2) It is important to remember that the Vietnam War was basically a struggle for independence. The Vietminh (Vietnamese who fought for independence) fought the Japanese, the French, and then the United States to achieve nationhood. American leaders even supported the Vietminh struggle at first. During World War II, the Vietminh and the American military worked together against the Japanese.[1] After World War II, the French moved back into Vietnam to retake control of their former colony. A war broke out between the Vietminh and the French. American leaders, remembering our

*[Continued on next page.]*

## Interpretation A

*[Continued from previous page.]*

own struggle for independence against the British, refused to aid the French.

(3) In 1950 America changed from this sensible policy. The "fall" of China to Communism, the Korean War, and the anti-communist charges by Senator Joseph McCarthy made American leaders paranoid about Communists.[2] The French argument that the Vietminh were Communists was now more convincing. By 1954 America was supplying the French with 80 percent of the cost of the Vietnam War.[3]

(4) The war went badly for the French. They were defeated in the May 1954 battle of Dien Bien Phu. They soon negotiated a peace settlement with the Vietminh at the Geneva Peace Conference. The country was *temporarily* divided. The French forces were to withdraw south of the 17th parallel and the Vietminh were to withdraw north of the line. The agreement further stated that there would be an election within two years to reunify the country.[4] Everyone agreed that the leader of the independence movement, Ho Chi Minh, would win that election.[5] He was the symbol of Vietnamese independence, just as George Washington represented American independence from England.

(5) At this point the United States could have stayed out of the situation and Vietnam would have become an independent Communist nation in 1956 under Ho Chi Minh. But the United States decided to intervene to stop the Vietminh.

(6) First, the United States made a military alliance called SEATO. According to the Geneva Conference, neither part of Vietnam could be part of an alliance. So the United States had "the free territory under the jurisdiction of Vietnam" added as a territory to be defended by the alliance.[6] The regroupment zone in the southern part of Vietnam, which was not a country and which did not participate in the SEATO talks, was made an honorary member of a military alliance!

(7) Second, the United States gave its backing to Ngo Dinh Diem as leader of a separate South Vietnamese government. Diem, who had been living in New Jersey up to 1954,[7] was viewed favorably by the United States since he also opposed the scheduled 1956 elections. In 1955 Diem, backed by American aid and in clear violation of the Geneva Agreement, declared that South Vietnam was a country, and stated that the nationwide elections would not be held.

(8) Diem was an oppressive ruler who created problems for himself by his foolish policies. First, he said that anyone who was or had been a Communist, or had associated with Communists could be thrown into jail. Anyone who had opposed French rule had associated with Communists in the Vietminh. Thus, any freedom-lover could now be thrown into jail! South Vietnam was a police state.[8]

(9) Second, Diem started a land reform program which "reduced" rents. But the peasants in Vietminh-controlled areas now owned their land (they paid no rent); the landlords had fled to the cities. The land reform program actually put many landlords back in control.[9] The South Vietnamese people hated these two policies.

(10) War again broke out, this time between the Vietcong (South Vietnamese who fought for independence) and Diem's authoritarian government. In 1960 the North Vietnamese began

*[Continued on next page.]*

## Interpretation A

*[Continued from previous page.]*

sending large amounts of aid to the Vietcong. The United States stepped up its military aid to the South Vietnamese government, and President Kennedy began sending American "advisers" to help the South Vietnamese military.

(11) By 1964 the United States could still have disengaged from Vietnam. The number of troops there was small—about 16,000—and few Americans had been killed, but President Johnson could not stand to see Vietnam become Communist. In the Gulf of Tonkin Resolution (1964), Congress agreed to let the president use "whatever means necessary" to stop Communist aggression in Vietnam. American troops could now fight. In 1965 large numbers of American troops were committed to the war. By 1968 over 500,000 American troops were in Vietnam. President Johnson also increased the amount of bombing. The United States had dropped over 6 million tons of bombs on Indochina (Vietnam, Laos, and Cambodia) by the end of the war, of which over 4 million fell on South Vietnam.[10] This is three times as much tonnage as was dropped by the United States in all of World War II.

(12) What did all these troops and bombings accomplish? Basically, they led to the destruction of Vietnamese society. Large numbers of innocent civilians were killed by American soldiers.[11] The My Lai Massacre was unusual because of the large number of civilians killed, but American soldiers killing civilians was not unusual. American generals emphasized number of enemy killed (called "body count"), rather than capture of territory. Officers were under pressure to get a high body count. This led to such expressions as, "If he's Vietnamese, and he's dead, he's Vietcong," and to the counting of bodies on the battlefield several times by different American troops. (For example, three dead bodies would lead to a count of three dead by the infantry, three by the artillery, and three by the Air Force.)

(13) Vietnamese civilians were also killed by bombings. From an airplane there is no possible way to separate civilians from guerrillas (which the Vietcong were), so large numbers of civilians had to be killed by the bombings. Each of the civilians killed had relatives who might then join the Vietcong out of hatred for the Americans.

(14) American firepower destroyed Vietnamese society and basically guaranteed we would lose the war. American generals did what they thought was best—use American weapons to defeat the enemy militarily. The problem was that the Vietnam War was a struggle for the hearts and minds of the Vietnamese peasants. You cannot win people over to your side by destroying their villages and killing their relatives. Our firepower continually created more enemies.

(15) Another way the United States could have disentangled itself from Vietnam was through a negotiated settlement between the Vietcong, the South Vietnamese Government, and the Buddhists. The Americans told the South Vietnamese not to negotiate.[12]

(16) No wonder American soldiers did not know what they were fighting for. There was no good reason for the fighting—we never should have become involved in Vietnam. Having continually lied to the American people about the war, the Johnson Administration was embarrassed by the unusual strength of the Vietcong in the 1968 Tet Offen-

*[Continued on next page.]*

## Interpretation A

*[Continued from previous page.]*

sive.[13] The Administration had said that the enemy was too weak to attack. American citizens wondered if government statements were truthful and began to protest against the war in large numbers. By 1973 the continuous protests gradually brought an end to the insanity of American involvement in the Vietnam War.

*(17)* The United States consciously became involved in a war in which it had no business. It tried to fight the political war by military firepower. But American firepower only made more Vietnamese join the guerrilla side. We could not win as long as most South Vietnamese supported the Vietcong. In the end, the American people forced the end of the useless killing in this needless war.

## *Endnotes for Interpretation A*

[1] Bernard Fall (historian), *The Two Viet Nams* (1964), pp. 100–101.

[2] Statement by President Truman linking aid to Vietnam with United States intervention in the Korean War. *Department of State Bulletin*, July 3, 1950, p. 5.

State Department Policy Statement on Indochina, September 27, 1948:

"We have not urged the French to negotiate with Ho Chi Minh, even though he probably is supported by a considerable majority of the Vietnamese people, because of his record as a Communist."

[3] *New York Times*, April 7, 1954.

[4] Geneva Agreements, 1954, paragraph 7.

[5] CIA (Central Intelligence Agency) National Intelligence Estimate, August 3, 1954:

"If the scheduled national elections are held in July 1956, and if the Viet Minh [sic.] does not prejudice its political prospects, the Viet Minh [sic.] will almost certainly win."

Also, Dwight David Eisenhower, *Mandate for Change* (1963), p. 372:

"I have never talked or corresponded with a person knowledgeable in Indochinese affairs who did not agree that had elections been held as of the time of the fighting, possibly 80 percent of the population would have voted for the Communist Ho Chi Minh."

[6] Southeast Asia Collective Defense Treaty, *Southeast Asia Treaty Organization*, Department of State Publication 6305 (1956). See especially "Protocol to the Southeast Asia Collective Defense Treaty."

[7] George Kahin and John Lewis (historians), *The United States in Vietnam* (1976), p. 66.

[8] P. J. Honey, "The Problem of Democracy in Vietnam," *The World Today*, Vol. 16, No. 2, February 1960, p. 73. On the basis of talks with former inmates of Diem's prison camps, he stated, "The majority of detainees are neither Communist nor pro-Communist."

Also, William Henderson, "South Viet Nam Finds Itself," *Foreign Affairs*, Vol. 35, No. 2, January 1957, pp. 285–88.

"South Viet Nam is today a quasi-police state characterized by arbitrary arrests and imprisonment."

[9] John D. Montgomery, The *Politics of Foreign Aid* (1962), p. 124:

"The Vietnamese government, not wishing to disturb the strong landowning classes, resisted the proposed transfers of land [to the peasants] and the sharper rent controls [lower than 25 percent]."

[10] Raphael Littauer and Norman Uphoff, ed. The *Air War in Indochina* (1972), Graph 11, Figure 1-1 "Annual Tonnage of Aerial Munitions, 1965–1971."

*[Continued on next page.]*

## Endnotes for Interpretation A
*[Continued from previous page.]*

[11] United States Senate, *United States Policy with Respect to Mainland China*, 89th Congress, 2nd Session (1966), p. 349. Also Kahin and Lewis, *United States in Vietnam*, p. 239:

"...the ratio of civilian to Vietcong casualties [was] reported as high as 2 to 1...."

[12] *New York Times*, November 10, 1964.

"...a negotiated settlement and neutralization of Vietnam are not to be ruled out."

Also, President Johnson's New Year's message to the government of South Vietnam, *New York Times*, January 1 and 2, 1964:

"Neutralization of South Vietnam would only be another name for a Communist take-over."

[13] *New York Times*, December 27, 1967, and February 13, 1968.

## Interpretation B

*(1)* The Vietnam War was a frustrating conflict for the United States. American soldiers won every battle, yet the Communists won the war. This frustration has led to a number of misinterpretations about this tragic event.

*(2)* Some historians blame the United States for almost every evil that took place during the war. The United States, they argue, had no legitimate reason for getting involved in the conflict from the beginning. Once we were involved, we incorrectly fought the war militarily and destroyed Vietnamese society with our bombing and other firepower. This viewpoint is wrong on every count.

*(3)* It is important to recognize that the United States had legitimate national interests in Vietnam. Our enemies were Communists (Ho Chi Minh had been a long-time member of the international Communist movement), and the Korean War showed that Communists were not afraid to try to take over other nations by force. Our aid to the French would help contain Communism.

*(4)* After the French were defeated at Dien Bien Phu in 1954, they negotiated the Geneva Agreement with the Vietminh Communists. Some historians argue that the Vietminh were cheated out of a legitimate victory by American and South Vietnamese violations of the Geneva Agreement. But the Agreement itself was never signed and not even adopted by a formal vote, so it was not much of an agreement. The nationwide election scheduled for 1956, which Ho Chi Minh would supposedly have won by a landslide, was not taken seriously by any country at the Conference because the agreement was full of contradictions.[1] For example, why would the Agreement allow people to escape from one zone (the North) to the other (the South), when the two zones would be reunified in 700 days? South Vietnam said it would not agree to the elections if the elections jeopardized its independence.[2] Moreover, Communists never hold free elections, so the whole idea was a sham. As John F. Kennedy stated in 1956:

Neither the United States nor Free Vietnam was a party to that agreement [on elections]—and neither the United States nor Free Vietnam is ever going to be a party to an election obviously stacked and subverted in advance, urged on up by those [the Communists] who have already broken their own pledges under the agreement they now seek to enforce.[3]

*[Continued on next page.]*

## Interpretation B

*[Continued from previous page.]*

(5) So Ngo Dinh Diem, South Vietnam's new leader, was indeed justified in declaring South Vietnam a separate nation and in saying that he would not allow the 1956 election to be held in South Vietnam. The majority of the people in South Vietnam wanted independence from North Vietnam.

(6) When the elections were not held, North Vietnam began to use force to take over South Vietnam. Some people have argued that the war in South Vietnam was fought by the Vietcong (National Liberation Front) which was independent of North Vietnam. In fact, North Vietnam controlled the war in South Vietnam from the start. The North Vietnamese created the NLF as a cover for their role in the war, and to prevent charges that they had invaded South Vietnam. North Vietnamese defectors found it humorous that Americans believed Communist propaganda.[4]

(7) The 1965 introduction of large numbers of American troops turned the tide in favor of the South Vietnamese Government. The effectiveness of American soldiers on the battlefield was undermined, however, by the lack of strategy on the part of American civilian leaders. What several presidents, but especially President Johnson, did was fail to resolve to fight to win the war. War is a serious matter. It requires the undivided attention of the President, the Congress, and the citizenry. The President, in particular, has the duty to define the aims of the war, fix a strategy for success, and clarify to the American people why they and their sons should be willing to sacrifice. President Johnson never confronted the American people with the reality of this choice.[5]

(8) Johnson was concerned about domestic politics, especially his Great Society program. Consequently, he sent in enough troops to avoid losing the war but not enough to win it. The Joint Chiefs of Staff protested, but Johnson was not listening. He had put civilian strategists in charge of the war. Their psychological strategy was to "calibrate" American bombing—increase it a little at a time to get the North Vietnamese to negotiate. The gradual increases in American bombing reduced their effectiveness by allowing the North Vietnamese to adjust gradually.

(9) Despite these limitations on the American military, there were several points at which the United States and South Vietnam were close to winning the war. In 1968 the Vietcong tried an all-out attack in the Tet Offensive. They were thoroughly defeated and effectively eliminated as a fighting force.[6] Without the Vietcong, the guerrilla war withered, and the North Vietnamese Army had to fight large-scale battles against the better-armed Americans and South Vietnamese. The advantage on the battlefield swung clearly to the United States side. Many Americans at home, however, withdrew their support for the war after the Tet Offensive. No one had told them why they were making such sacrifices in Vietnam. With no overall goals or strategy for the war, Americans could not see why we should keep fighting. The American people forced Johnson to start withdrawing troops precisely when our military leaders were saying that more troops and an offensive strategy would bring us victory.

(10) The Communists again made a desperate gamble when they invaded South Vietnam in the 1972 Easter Offensive. They were thrown back by the South Vietnamese Army (most Ameri-

*[Continued on next page.]*

## Interpretation B

*[Continued from previous page.]*

can troops were out of Vietnam by 1972) with losses of over 130,000 men.[7] So the North Vietnamese switched strategy. They decided to win at the negotiating table what they had failed to win on the battlefield. The Nixon Administration could have decided on a tough policy in order to achieve victory. By this time, however, seven years after the introduction of large numbers of American troops, support for the war had vanished. Our leaders had to negotiate. Henry Kissinger won the Nobel Peace Prize for negotiating the 1973 Paris Peace Agreement, but it sold out South Vietnam. The North Vietnamese were allowed to keep their army in South Vietnam while the United States forces were withdrawn. Meanwhile, the Communists agreed to return American prisoners of war (POWs).[8] The Communists used the breather provided by the agreement to build up their army for the final attack in 1975 in which they took over South Vietnam.

*(11)* It is curious that American reporters criticized the American military for committing atrocities in Vietnam while dismissing the barbarity of the Communists. There should be no mistaking the nature of warfare—it is brutal. American soldiers were heavily armed and made lavish use of their firepower. Some soldiers committed crimes, but they were tried in military courts. American bombing was extremely heavy. Most of the tonnage was dropped in the lightly populated jungle, however, so few civilians were killed.

*(12)* The Communists, meanwhile, used systematic terror to control the population. From the start, the North Vietnamese Government was as totalitarian and oppressive as any government in the world. North Vietnamese people had almost no rights. People who op-

posed the Communists or their programs were executed. At least 50,000 (estimates go as high as 500,000) North Vietnamese died in the Communist "land reform" program alone.[9] Over 1 million people escaped from North Vietnam after 1954 to get away from Communist oppression.

*(13)* The Vietcong used terror and executions (several thousand per year) to intimidate the population of South Vietnam. The American media seemed to pay scant attention to the Vietcong atrocity in Dak San, where the Communists used flamethrowers to burn the residents to death. There was very little in the American press about the mass grave of 5,700 civilians killed at Hue by the Vietcong in the 1968 Tet Offensive. In captured documents, the Vietcong gloated over the executions, lamenting only that they couldn't have killed more people.[10]

*(14)* Some observers believe that the United States lost the Vietnam War because we fought it militarily, that the real struggle was for the allegiance of the South Vietnamese people. The more people we bombed, they argue, the more enemy guerrillas we created. This argument is refuted by the fact that South Vietnam was defeated by a conventional military invasion, not by a guerrilla takeover. Winning hearts and minds had less to do with victory in Vietnam than tanks and artillery.

*(15)* In the Vietnam war the United States was trying to protect the independence of a free people from an invasion by a determined and brutal enemy. The American military did its job admirably—winning every battle. What was missing was a decision by our civilian leaders to focus the national will

*[Continued on next page.]*

## Interpretation B

*[Continued from previous page.]*

and determination on the fight. We needed to decide as a nation whether the sacrifice was worth it. Instead, President Johnson tried to fight the war secretly, with no national debate. As time wore on, Americans lost interest in what they saw as a needless meatgrinder chewing up our young men and resources. They had no clear idea of why the country was fighting. In the end, our determined enemy simply outlasted us. The tragedy is not that America fought in Vietnam. The tragedy is that we fought the war without the determination to fight it to victory.

## *Endnotes for Interpretation B*

[1] Guenter Lewy (historian), *America in Vietnam* (1978), p. 8.

[2] Summarized from a statement by the South Vietnamese delegate to the Geneva Conference, *Documents on American Foreign Relations*, Council of Foreign Relations (1955), pp. 315–16.

[3] Speech to Friends of Vietnam, quoted in Hans J. Morgenthau (historian), "The 1954 Geneva Conference: An Assessment," *America's Stake in Vietnam* (1956), p. 13.

[4] Jeffrey Race, *War Comes to Long An: Revolutionary Conflict in a Vietnamese Province* (1972), pp. 107, 122:

> "They [two Communist defectors whom he interviewed] both commented humorously that the [Communist] Party [of North Vietnam] had apparently been more successful than was expected in concealing its role [in the war in South Vietnam]."

> "[Another defector said]...The Central Committee could hardly permit the International Control Commission to say that there was an invasion from the North, so it was necessary to have some name [the NLF]...to clothe these forces with some political organization."

[5] Former Secretary of State Dean Rusk stated in 1976, "We never made any effort to create a war psychology in the United States during the Vietnam affair. We didn't have military parades through cities...."

[6] "Conduct of the War in Vietnam," A report commissioned in 1971 by the United States Army Deputy Chief of Staff for Military Operations. (Summary from Reference Document I, not a direct quotation).

> "The number of attacks by enemy battalions or larger forces dropped from 16 per month in the first half of 1968 [before the Tet Offensive] to less than 5 per month in the second half of 1968 [after the Tet Offensive]."

See also Sir Robert Thompson, *Peace is Not at Hand* (1974), Chapter 5.

[7] Thompson, *Peace*, Chapter 6.

[8] Douglas Pike, "The Other Side," *The Wilson Quarterly*, Vol VII, No. 3, Summer, 1983, p. 124.

[9] Bernard Fall, *The Two Viet Nams: A Political and Military Analysis* (1967), p. 156.

[10] Robert F. Turner, *Vietnamese Communism: Its Origins and Development* (1975), p. 251.

> A captured Vietcong document stated that at Hue the Communists: "...eliminated 1,892 administrative personnel, 38 policemen, 790 tyrants."

*[Continued on next page.]*

*[Continued from previous page.]*

## Relevant Information

1.  Public statement by Dean Acheson, Secretary of State, February 1, 1950:

    "The recognition by the Kremlin (U.S.S.R.) of Ho Chi Minh's Communist movement in Indochina comes as a surprise. The Soviet acknowledgment of this movement should remove any illusions as to the "nationalist" nature of Ho Chi Minh's aims and reveal Ho in his true colors as the mortal enemy of native independence in Indochina."

2.  United States Consul in Saigon, George Abbott, February 12, 1949:

    "One peculiar thing about Vietnam Communism is that there has been very little anti-American propaganda."

3.  Public statement by Robert McNamara, Secretary of Defense, March 26, 1964:

    "Thus today in Vietnam we are not dealing with factional disputes or the remnants of a colonial struggle against the French but rather with a major test case of Communism's new strategy."

4.  Edward Doyle, et al., *Passing the Torch,* Vol. 2 of *The Vietnam Experience* (1981), p. 146:

    "A 1956 presidential ordinance [by Diem] authorizing the arrest and detention in political re-education centers 'of all persons deemed dangerous to the state' inflicted hardship and suffering on tens of thousands of people, Communists and non-Communists alike. It did, however, succeed in decimating the Communist party structure in the South. By the summer of 1956, approximately 90 percent of all [Communist] cells had been smashed in one province; other provinces showed similar results."

5.  Roger Hilsman, State Department, Research Memorandum for the Secretary of State, December 3, 1962:

    "The extensive use of artillery and aerial bombardment and other apparently excessive and indiscriminate measures by GVN [Government of South Vietnam] military and security forces in attempting to eliminate the Viet Cong have undoubtedly killed many innocent peasants and made many others more willing than before to cooperate with the Viet Cong."

## Worksheet for Lesson 22

 ### Interpretation A

1.  What is the main point of the argument in Interpretation A?

*[Continued on next page.]*

*[Continued from previous page.]*

2.  Identify and evaluate the reasoning used in paragraph 4, when the author talks about Ho Chi Minh and George Washington.

3.  Evaluate the evidence in endnote 5.

4.  Restate the argument made in paragraphs 4 and 6 in Interpretation A regarding the nationwide 1956 election in "premise, premise, conclusion" form. Remember to state the second premise in general terms: "People who —."

    Premise:

    Premise:

    Conclusion:

5.  Evaluate the above argument.

6.  Evaluate the cause-and-effect reasoning used in paragraph 8, paragraph 9, and the first sentence of paragraph 12 in Interpretation A.

7.  Write down and evaluate one sentence in paragraph 10 which uses generalization reasoning.

*[Continued on next page.]*

*[Continued from previous page.]*

8.   What is a possible weakness in paragraph 16?

**Q**   Interpretation B

9.   What is the main point of the argument in Interpretation B?

10.   What is the primary type of reasoning used in paragraph 2 of Interpretation B?

11.   Evaluate the evidence in paragraph 4 referenced as endnote 1.

12.   Evaluate the argument in paragraph 6.

13.   What unstated assumption is made in paragraph 8 about civilian leaders in war? Do you agree with it? Why or why not?

*[Continued on next page.]*

*[Continued from previous page.]*

14. Evaluate the proof-by-evidence reasoning used from the beginning of paragraph 9 to the marker for endnote 6.

15. Evaluate the evidence in endnote 10.

16. Evaluate the argument in paragraph 14.

## Q Relevant Information

17. Identify one piece of relevant information and explain how it affects one or both of the viewpoints presented.

# OPINION SURVEY ON WAR

| | STATEMENT | STRONGLY AGREE | AGREE | NEUTRAL | DISAGREE | STRONGLY DISAGREE | REASONS |
|---|---|---|---|---|---|---|---|
| 1 | It is wrong for the United States to support corrupt dictatorships in an effort to stop Communism. | | | | | | |
| 2 | Military leaders should be in charge of military strategy in a war. | | | | | | |
| 3 | Bombing of civilians in wartime is always wrong. | | | | | | |
| 4 | It is immoral for a country to enter a war without the intention of making the necessary sacrifices to win that war. | | | | | | |
| 5 | If guerrillas mix with the civilian population, then it is justifiable to kill some of the civilians in trying to kill the guerrillas. | | | | | | |
| 6 | Limited wars with limited objectives are sometimes necessary. For example, a country might fight a war to defend the independence of one country without attacking any other countries. | | | | | | |
| 7 | When a country has no national interest at stake in an area, it should not fight a war in that area. | | | | | | |
| 8 | The United States should not get involved in civil wars. | | | | | | |
| 9 | When a country's freedom is threatened by invasion or subversion, the United States should protect that country. | | | | | | |
| 10 | Since America once fought a revolution for independence, it should not oppose colonial struggles for independence today. | | | | | | |
| 11 | If the majority of people in a country choose Communism, then the United States has no business fighting Communism there. | | | | | | |

# Modern American Society and Politics

**LESSON 23**     Evaluating Evidence on McCarthyism and the
                  Red Scare

 Evaluate the following pieces of evidence by explaining their strengths and weaknesses. If you need help, refer to the section on **Evidence** in the "Guide to Critical Thinking" (Unit 1).

1.  Senator Joseph McCarthy, in a 1950 speech to the Republican Women's Club in Wheeling, West Virginia, claims that there are Communists in government. He states, "I have here in my hand a list of 205—a list of names that were made known to the Secretary of State as being members of the Communist party and who, nevertheless, are still working and shaping policy in the State Department." (Note: Evaluate the evidence by McCarthy, not the list.)

    STRENGTHS:                    WEAKNESSES:

2.  Roy Cohn, an aide to Joseph McCarthy, says in a magazine article that the Senator has been unfairly attacked for his attempts to catch Communists in (United States) government. Actually, the Senator is sincere in his efforts to help our country, Cohn says.

    STRENGTHS:                    WEAKNESSES:

3.  Three friends of Senator McCarthy say they met with him for lunch at the Colonial Restaurant in January 1950, about one month before McCarthy began accusing people of being Communists. At lunch they discussed possible campaign issues to help get McCarthy reelected. The St. Lawrence Seaway, as well as another issue, was rejected before they all agreed that Communism would be an ideal campaign issue.

    STRENGTHS:                    WEAKNESSES:

*[Continued on next page.]*

*[Continued from previous page.]*

4. In his 1973 book *The Unfinished Century: America Since 1900*, William E. Leuchtenburg says that, as a Senator, Joseph McCarthy was a bully who continually broke Senate rules and made vicious verbal attacks on other people.

    STRENGTHS:                    WEAKNESSES:

5. Earl Browder, the head of the Communist party of the United States, said that he had never met with or talked to Owen Lattimore in his life, implying that Lattimore had never been a member of the Communist party. Browder was testifying under oath before a Senate Committee investigating Senator McCarthy's charges that Communists, including Lattimore, worked for the government. Lattimore had previously said that he talked with Browder in 1937.

    STRENGTHS:                    WEAKNESSES:

6. In 1952 government officials searched a suspected Communist's barn and found secret letters and other documents. One letter, from the early 1940s, was written by Owen Lattimore. In it, he told a friend that he worked regularly at a desk at the State Department. (Lattimore told a Senate Committee in 1951 that he had never had a desk and had never worked at the State Department on a regular basis.)

    STRENGTHS:                    WEAKNESSES:

7. Whittaker Chambers, a former member of the Communist party, told a House Committee that Alger Hiss, a former member of the State Department, had been a member of the Communist party and a spy.

    STRENGTHS:                    WEAKNESSES:

# LESSON 24    Analyzing Cause and Effect on Urban Riots

**Q** Decide which of the following situations would lead to a riot and which would not. Give reasons for your choices. The situations are real.

| Situation | Would lead to a riot | Would not lead to a riot |
|---|---|---|
| 1. In New York City on July 16, 1964, several young blacks walking to summer school classes became involved in an argument with a white building superintendent. An off-duty police lieutenant got involved. | | |
| **Reasons** | | |
| 2. On August 15, 1964, when a white liquor store owner in the Chicago suburb of Dixmore had a black woman arrested for stealing a bottle of whiskey, he was accused of having manhandled her. | | |
| **Reasons** | | |
| 3. In Philadelphia, during the summer of 1964, a black couple's car stalled at an intersection in an area known as "the Jungle"—an area which, with almost 2000 persons living in each block, has the greatest incidence of crime, disease, unemployment, and poverty in the city. When two police officers, one white and one black, attempted to move the car, the wife became abusive and the officers arrested her. | | |
| **Reasons** | | |
| 4. On August 11, 1965, Los Angeles sweltered in a heat wave. A patrolman halted a young black man for speeding. The young man appeared intoxicated and the patrolman arrested him. | | |
| **Reasons** | | |

*[Continued from previous page.]*

## Connection between Cause and Effect

In 1965, 1966, and 1967, there were numerous riots by blacks in the slums of major United States cities, including Los Angeles, Chicago, Detroit, Cleveland, New York, and Newark. These riots did millions of dollars worth of damage and left hundreds dead and thousands injured. In 1968 a report was issued on the cause of the riots. The following three arguments all say that poverty was the main cause of the riots.

**Q** Read the arguments, then decide which argument is strongest and explain why you think so. The key question to be answered here is "How well does each historian explain the connection between the cause (poverty) and the effect (riot)?"

### Historian A

The urban riots by blacks were mainly caused by poverty in the slums. Blacks were so poor they had no hope. In this hopeless state, blacks attacked department stores, grocery stores, and liquor stores—in fact, almost any type of business. In Watts (a section of Los Angeles), 34 people were killed, hundreds were wounded, and there was $35 million in damage. In Detroit, 43 people were killed, 2000 injured, and more than 4000 fires burned a large part of the city. After flying in a helicopter over the smoking ruins, Michigan Governor George Romney said that Detroit looked like "a city that has been bombed."

### Historian B

The 1960's urban riots by blacks were mainly caused by poverty in the slums. Blacks had an unemployment rate three times higher than that of whites, and blacks who did work generally made low wages. Meanwhile, television reminded blacks of all the things they did not own and could not get. With a lot of bored, frustrated people hanging around, the slightest incident, such as an arrest, could create a mob where rioting against "the system," and looting to get the things blacks could never afford to buy, was natural.

### Historian C

The 1960's urban riots by blacks were mainly caused by poverty in the slums. Blacks were much worse off than most whites, especially those whites who lived in suburbs. Many blacks rented, rather than owned, their homes. When repairs were needed, black tenants had to wait until the landlord (usually white) decided

*[Continued on next page.]*

## Historian C

*[Continued from previous page.]*

to fix things. Many of the apartments were overcrowded which led to further decay of the buildings. Roofs and plumbing leaked, plaster broke, and insects wandered about. Given these conditions, frustration was inevitable and this frustration led to the riots.

5. Which of the three arguments is strongest? Why do you think so? (This question is asking which argument makes the strongest connection between the cause and the effect.)

## Commission Report

After the 1960's inner city riots began, President Johnson appointed a commission to study the causes of these riots and to recommend actions to correct the situation. On March 1, 1968, the National Advisory Commission on Civil Disorders reported on the riots. What follows is a short section of their report.

> This is our basic conclusion: Our nation is moving toward two societies, one black, one white, separate and unequal....
>
> Violence and destruction must be ended, in the streets of the ghetto and in the lives of the people. Segregation and poverty have created in the racial ghetto a destructive environment totally unknown to most white Americans. What white Americans have never fully understood, but what the Negro can never forget, is that white society is deeply implicated in the ghetto. White institutions created it, white institutions maintain it, and white society condones it....
>
> White racism is essentially responsible for the explosive mixture which has been accumulating in our cities since the end of World War II....
>
> Frustrated hopes are the residue of the unfulfilled expectations aroused by the great judicial and legislative victories for the civil rights movement and the dramatic struggle for equal rights in the South.
>
> A climate that tends toward approval and encouragement of violence as a form of protest has been created by white terrorism directed against nonviolent protest; by the open defiance of law and federal authority by state and local officials resisting desegregation; and by some protest groups engaging in civil disobedience.
>
> [W]e propose the following objectives for national action:
>
> Opening up opportunities to those who are restricted by racial segregation and discrimination and eliminating all barriers to their choice of jobs, education, and housing....

*[Continued on next page.]*

*[Continued from previous page.]*

6. Evaluate the Commission's cause-and-effect reasoning.

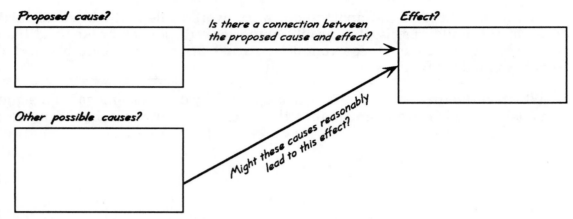

Overall, how strong is the Commission's reasoning?

7. According to the Commission, how can the riots be stopped? What do you think of its recommendations?

# LESSON 25     Identifying and Evaluating Types of Reasoning

 Identify the type of reasoning used in each item below, then evaluate it by asking and answering the appropriate question(s). Each item may contain more than one type of reasoning. Focus your evaluation on the type of reasoning that is most central to the argument. Make diagrams to assist your evaluation when you think they would be helpful. The types of reasoning are listed below. Appropriate questions for evaluating each type of reasoning can be found in the "Guide to Critical Thinking" (Unit 1, pp. 5, 8, 10, 11, 13).

| | |
|---|---|
| Cause and Effect | Proof by Eliminating Alternatives |
| Generalization | Proof by Evidence |
| Comparison | |

1. In 1987 a school superintendent wrote a letter to the striking teachers in his district. In it he said that if the majority of teachers followed the union leaders in the strike, they were choosing the position of the majority of German citizens in the 1930s and '40s who looked the other way when the Nazis began the genocide of the Jews.

   Type of Reasoning:


   Evaluation:


2. Christine and Leanne are the only ones who could ride such a small bike, but Leanne was gone all day, so Christine must have been the one who borrowed it.

   Type of Reasoning:


   Evaluation:


*[Continued on next page.]*

*[Continued from previous page.]*

3. President Eisenhower was a conservative (opposed to government measures, such as the New Deal), but he was a practical man. He saw that New Deal programs were still popular in the 1950s, so he supported the programs.

Type of Reasoning:

Evaluation:

4. Senator Joseph McCarthy's charges that there were security risks (people of questionable loyalty) in government were correct. Twenty-nine percent of the people he accused were later fired.

Type of Reasoning:

Evaluation:

5. According to *Time* magazine, 40% of welfare recipients in 1987 stayed on welfare more than three years, while the average stay on welfare was a little over two years.

Type of Reasoning:

Evaluation:

6. Governor Orval Faubus opposed integration in Little Rock, Arkansas, in 1957 because he needed the white segregationist (people opposed to integration) vote in the upcoming election. He was also encouraged to resist because political leaders in other southern states had signed a document saying they would resist integration.

Type of Reasoning:

Evaluation:

*[Continued on next page.]*

*[Continued from previous page.]*

7. "The stock market crash of October 1987 is even larger than the crash of October 1929, so we should have a depression any time." (Statement made in December 1987)

   Type of Reasoning:

   Evaluation:

8. "It's a crime for an individual to relieve himself or herself in a river. Amazingly, however, it is not a crime for a corporation to relieve itself in a river. We must stop corporate polluters." (Statement by an environmentalist in the 1970s)

   Type of Reasoning:

   Evaluation:

9. Richard Nixon won decisively over Hubert Humphrey in the electoral vote in 1968, 301 to 191. But he won by the slightest of margins in the popular vote, 31.8 million to 31.3 million for Humphrey.

   Type of Reasoning:

   Evaluation:

10. "Welfare benefits are unfair. In Alabama a family of three gets $4000 a year in AFDC (Aid to Families with Dependent Children) and food stamp benefits. Meanwhile, in Alaska such a family gets about $11,500." (Argument made in 1987)

   Type of Reasoning:

   Evaluation:

## LESSON 26    Types of Reasoning about Civil Rights

This lesson contains a number of statements and summaries of statements concerning civil rights. Read the statements and answer the questions which follow them.

 Read the following summary of reasoning used in the 1954 Supreme Court case *Brown v. Board of Education* and answer the questions.

> The case *Plessy v. Ferguson* in 1896 declared that separate facilities for blacks and whites could be equal. But *Plessy v. Ferguson* dealt with transportation, not education. Testimony in this case shows that separate schools for blacks and whites are not equal. Psychological experts stated that separate schools make blacks feel inferior. Separate schools are inherently unequal and thus violate the equal protection clause of the Fourteenth Amendment of the Constitution.

1. What is the conclusion?

_____ 2.    What are the Justices doing in the second sentence?

A. Attacking the sample in sentence 1.

B. Questioning the evidence in sentence 1.

C. Showing that the comparison in sentence 1 is weak.

D. Substituting cause-and-effect reasoning for the debating reasoning in sentence 1.

_____ 3.    The phrase "Testimony in this case shows..." indicates what type of reasoning?

A. Comparison

B. Proof by Evidence

C. Proof by Authority

D. Sample

E. Cause and Effect

*[Continued on next page.]*

*[Continued from previous page.]*

_____ 4. The phrase "Psychological experts testified..." indicates what type of reasoning?

A. Comparison

B. Cause and Effect

C. Proof by Authority

D. Debating

_____ 5. The phrase "...separate schools make blacks feel inferior" indicates what type of reasoning?

A. Comparison

B. Cause and Effect

C. Proof by Authority

D. Proof by Evidence

**Q** In March of 1956, about two years after *Brown v. Board of Education*, nineteen southern Senators and seventy-seven southern Congressmen explained their opposition to the decision in a statement known as "The Southern Manifesto." Read the following summary of "The Southern Manifesto" and answer the questions.

> We regard the decision of the Supreme Court in the school cases as a clear abuse of judicial power. The Court has wrongfully exercised powers that were reserved to the States in the Tenth Amendment of the Constitution.
>
> The original Constitution does not mention education. Neither does the Fourteenth Amendment, nor any other Amendment. Further, in case after case, the doctrine of "separate but equal" facilities, as provided by the States, has been upheld.
>
> The Supreme Court, nevertheless, substituted its own personal political and social beliefs in place of the established legal principle of control of education by the States. This is an unwarranted exercise of power by the Court and is creating chaos and confusion in the States principally affected.
>
> We pledge ourselves to use all lawful means to bring about a reversal of this decision which is contrary to the Constitution.

_____ 6. The sentence "The original Constitution does not mention education" indicates what type of reasoning?

A. Comparison

B. Cause and Effect

C. Generalization

D. Proof by Evidence

_____ 7. The argument that the principle of "separate but equal" had been upheld in "case after case" (and is therefore a good principle) is primarily what type of reasoning?

A. Comparison

B. Cause and Effect

C. Generalization

D. Proof by Eliminating Alternatives

*[Continued on next page.]*

*[Continued from previous page.]*

_____8.    The argument that the Supreme Court decision is "creating chaos and confusion in the States" is primarily what type of reasoning?

A. Comparison

B. Cause and Effect

C. Generalization

D. Proof by Eliminating Alternatives

9. What effects do you think this Manifesto, and especially the last paragraph, had on the situation in the Southern states regarding Civil Rights? Why do you think so?

**Q** After Rosa Parks was arrested in December 1955, blacks in Montgomery, Alabama, organized a 381-day bus boycott. The boycott was very effective; buses rolled through Montgomery nearly empty. The bus company almost went bankrupt.

_____10.    This argument implies that very few blacks rode the buses during the boycott. What type of reasoning is this?

A. Comparison

B. Cause and Effect

C. Generalization

D. Proof by Authority

_____11.    Primarily what type of reasoning is used in the argument that the bus company almost went bankrupt due to the bus boycott?

A. Comparison

B. Cause and Effect

C. Generalization

D. Proof by Authority

12. Evaluate the argument given in question 11 that the bus company almost went bankrupt due to the bus boycott.

*[Continued on next page.]*

*[Continued from previous page.]*

 Martin Luther King was the Gandhi of the Civil Rights Movement. Like Gandhi, King used nonviolent resistance to win his opponents over through love.

_____13.    What type of reasoning does this argument primarily use?

A.  Comparison

B.  Cause and Effect

C.  Generalization

D.  Proof by Eliminating Alternatives

14.  Evaluate the argument.

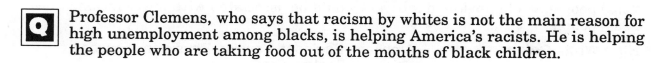 Professor Clemens, who says that racism by whites is not the main reason for high unemployment among blacks, is helping America's racists. He is helping the people who are taking food out of the mouths of black children.

_____15.    Which of the following is a possible fallacy in this argument?

A.  Stereotyping (p. 10)

B.  Hasty Generalization (p. 10)

C.  Numbers (p. 12)

D.  False Scenario (p. 6)

E.  Irrelevant Proof (p. 12)

## LESSON 27    Why Did Blacks Have Less Upward Mobility Than Immigrants in Boston from 1880 to 1970?

From 1880 to 1970, blacks in Boston had significantly less upward mobility than immigrants. That is, given a certain time period after moving to Boston, say forty years, blacks did not move up in class (especially in job levels) as much as immigrants did.

Below are several explanations by historians of why blacks did not do as well in improving their job categories as immigrants did after they migrated to Boston. Following these explanations is some information, mostly in the form of tables, which may be relevant to the question. Use this information to decide which of the historians' views is the best and explain why.

### Examples of Job Categories in 1970

From: Stephen Thernstrom, *The Other Bostonians: Poverty and Progress in the American Metropolis, 1880–1970.*

White collar jobs tend to be associated with higher income (middle and upper class) people, while unskilled laborers would be associated with lower income (lower class) people.

| | |
|---|---|
| **High White Collar** | Architect, Engineer, Lawyer, Physician, Teacher, Scientist, Banker, Broker |
| **Low White Collar** | Clerk, Sales, Accountant, Bank teller, Bookkeeper, Cashier, Insurance sales, Mail carrier |
| **Skilled Blue Collar** | Baker, Carpenter, Firefighter, Jeweler, Plumber, Machinist |
| **Semi-skilled and Service (Blue Collar)** | Barber, Bartender, Cook, Janitor, Servant, Gas station attendant, Waitperson, Delivery person |
| **Unskilled and Menial Service (Blue Collar)** | Gardener, Laborer, Lumberjack, Porter, Housekeeper |

### Theory A

Blacks did poorly when they migrated to Boston mainly because they came from the rural South. They were unprepared for urban life, so they could not take advantage of those opportunities to move up which were available. The city life of Boston was simply too complex and too different from life in the rural South, especially because the early black migrants came from families that had lived under slavery.

*[Continued on next page.]*

*[Continued from previous page.]*

## Theory B

The main reason for the poor performance of blacks in terms of mobility is due to the prejudice of whites in Boston. Whites in Boston had more prejudice against blacks than they had against any immigrant group.

## Theory C

Blacks did worse than immigrants in moving up on the job scale mainly because they were less interested in education. Black children did not go to school as long as whites, so how could they expect to better themselves in the job market?

## Theory D

Blacks did poorly in the job market mainly because they were concentrated, isolating themselves in ghettoes. Thus, they had less contact with others in the city. When opportunities for better jobs opened up, the employers did not know any blacks to hire, and the blacks had no way to find out about the jobs.

## Theory E

Larger families account for why blacks did not do as well as immigrants in improving themselves in the job market. With larger families, blacks could provide neither the same education nor the same financial help as they could have for fewer children. With this handicapped start, black children could not improve themselves as much as white children could.

## Theory F

The black family in Boston, as elsewhere, was disorganized and unstable. Just look at the statistics. In 1970 barely half (50.3 percent) of the black children in Boston were living with both of their parents. It has been established that a "background of living in a broken family hurts educational achievement." With less education, it is to be expected that blacks will do worse in occupational achievement.

## Theory G

Black culture is the main reason for the poor record of gains for blacks in Boston. This culture made blacks less qualified for better jobs than whites, and prevented blacks from seeing and taking advantage of job opportunities that were available to them.

*[Continued on next page.]*

*[Continued from previous page.]*

## Relevant Information

**Table 1**     Relative segregation in housing of blacks and first-generation immigrants, 1880–1950.

| Group | 1880 | 1910 | 1930 | 1940 |
|---|---|---|---|---|
| Black | 51 | 64 | 78 | 80 |
| English | 13 | 11 | 15 | 19 |
| German | 31 | 31 | 35 | 31 |
| Irish | 15 | 19 | 26 | 24 |
| Italian | 74 | 66 | 54 | 48 |
| Swedish | 27 | 23 | 32 | 31 |
| Russian (mostly Jewish) | 55 | 48 | 65 | 65 |

Note:  In Table 1, higher numbers mean greater segregation; 100 would mean all the people of that group live in areas that do not have any other ethnic groups living there, 0 means the people of that group are spread equally throughout the city's neighborhoods.

**Table 2**     Educational attainments of blacks and other groups, 1900–1970.

I     Percent attending school, 1900

| Age | Immigrant | Second-generation Immigrant | Native White | Black |
|---|---|---|---|---|
| 10–14 | 80% | 92% | 94% | 89% |
| 15–20 | 7 | 23 | 39 | 20 |

II     School years completed (percent), 1950

| School Years | Immigrant | Native White | Black |
|---|---|---|---|
| 6 or less | 41% | 6% | 26% |
| 7–8 | 36 | 31 | 39 |
| 9–11 | 9 | 21 | 15 |
| 12 or more | 13 | 42 | 20 |
| **Median Years** | 7.5 years | 10.8 years | 8.5 years |

*[Continued on next page.]*

*[Continued from previous page.]*

III      School years completed and occupational level (percent), 1950

|  | Irish | Italian | French-Canadian | Black |
|---|---|---|---|---|
| **Median School Years** | 8.4 years | 6.1 years | 8.5 years | 9.5 years |
| **Occupational Level** |  |  |  |  |
| **White-collar** | 19% | 19% | 20% | 15% |
| **Skilled** | 21 | 25 | 39 | 13 |
| **Low Manual** | 60 | 56 | 41 | 72 |

IV      Median school years of blacks relative to total population, 1940–1970

| Year | Median School Years | | Black Median as percent of City Median |
|---|---|---|---|
|  | **Total Population** | **Blacks** |  |
| **1940** | 8.9 years | 8.3 years | 93% |
| **1950** | 11.8 | 9.5 | 81% |
| **1960** | 12.1 | 10.5 | 87% |
| **1970** | 12.4 | 11.6 | 94% |

Note:  The median shows that half of the group went more and half went less than this number of years.

**Table 3**      Percent of families of blacks throughout Boston and various groups in specific areas of Boston with females as head of household, 1880.

| Families | % with Female Head of Household |
|---|---|
| Blacks (all of Boston) | 16% |
| South Boston (largely Irish) | 18 |
| Back Bay (mixed area—many wealthy residents) | 22 |
| Dorchester (mixed immigrants) | 19 |
| South End (largely Irish) | 27 |

*[Continued on next page.]*

*[Continued from previous page.]*

**Table 4**   Occupational distribution (percent) of black males, 1880–1900.

| Year | Place of Birth | Occupational Level | | |
|---|---|---|---|---|
| | | **White Collar** | **Skilled** | **Low Manual** |
| **1880** | North | 9% | 19% | 73% |
| | South | 7 | 9 | 84 |
| | Foreign | 7 | 12 | 81 |
| **1900** | Massachusetts | 12% | 14% | 74% |
| | Other North | 6 | 11 | 83 |
| | South | 8 | 12 | 80 |
| | Foreign | 6 | 16 | 78 |

**Table 5**   Occupational distribution (percent) of first-generation immigrant males over the age of 45, by nationality, 1950.

| Occupation | New England Native | Nationality of First-Generation Male Immigrants | | | | | |
|---|---|---|---|---|---|---|---|
| | | **English** | **Irish** | **Swedish** | **German** | **Russian (mostly Jewish)** | **Italian** |
| **White-collar** | 48% | 52% | 18% | 16% | 40% | 53% | 18% |
| **Blue-collar** | 52 | 48 | 82 | 84 | 60 | 46 | 82 |

**Table 6**   Occupational distribution (percent) of Irish and black males by generation, 1880.

| Ethnicity | White-collar | Skilled | Low manual |
|---|---|---|---|
| First generation * | | | |
| Irish | 12% | 21% | 67% |
| Black | 7 | 9 | 84 |
| Second generation ** | | | |
| Irish | 24 | 24 | 52 |
| Black | 9 | 19 | 73 |

\* First generation—born elsewhere (for Blacks, born in the South), moved to Boston
\** Second generation—born in Boston

*[Continued on next page.]*

*[Continued from previous page.]*

**Table 7**     Percent of black and white children living with both parents

| Year | Blacks | Whites |
|------|--------|--------|
| 1970 | 50.3%  | 87.9%  |

**Table 8**     Occupational distribution (percent) of blacks and immigrants, 1890, 1910, 1930

| Year | Ethnicity | Occupational Level | | |
|------|-----------|--------------|---------|------------|
|      |           | **White Collar** | **Skilled** | **Low Manual** |
| **1890** | First-generation immigrant | 18% | 37% | 45% |
|      | Second-generation immigrant | 32 | 34 | 34 |
|      | Black | 8 | 11 | 81 |
| **1910** | First-generation immigrant | 24% | 33% | 43% |
|      | Second-generation immigrant | 45 | 21 | 34 |
|      | Black | 10 | 8 | 82 |
| **1930** | First-generation immigrant | 24% | 30% | 46% |
|      | Second-generation immigrant* | N/A | N/A | N/A |
|      | Blacks | 11 | 12 | 77 |

\* No information on occupations of second-generation immigrants was given for 1930.

**Table 9**     Fertility (number of children ever born) of women in Boston, aged 35–44.

| Year | Black Women | All Women |
|------|-------------|-----------|
| **1960** | 2.35 | 2.58 |
| **1970** | 3.41 | 3.16 |

*[Continued on next page.]*

*[Continued from previous page.]*

**Table 10**   Index of relative occupational concentration of blacks, 1900, 1940, 1950.

| Occupation | 1900 | 1940 | 1950 |
|---|---|---|---|
| Unskilled and menial service | 347 | 365 | 366 |
| Semiskilled operative | 24 | 63 | 117 |

Note:   The index is compared to the population as a whole—100 means there was the same percentage of blacks in an occupation as for the population as a whole, higher than 100 means a higher concentration, and lower than 100 means a lower concentration.

**Table 11**   Infant mortality (percent of children who died before reaching age 1).

| Year | Blacks | Whites |
|---|---|---|
| 1900 | 32% | 19% |

12.   Unskilled and menial service jobs are traditionally "Negro" jobs. Semiskilled operative jobs demanded no more skills than the "Negro" jobs. In 1940 there was a sudden demand for semiskilled jobs because of World War II.

13.   Whites in the same income levels as blacks in 1960 had significantly higher job levels (more white collar jobs, etc.).

14.   Blacks had about the same percentage of broken families as whites with the same income level in 1960.

*[Continued on next page.]*

*[Continued from previous page.]*

**Q** Evaluate the viewpoints of the historians.

| Historian | Relevant information which affects this interpretation | Overall judgment of the viewpoint |
|---|---|---|
| A (p. 144) | | |
| B (p. 145) | | |
| C (p. 145) | | |
| D (p. 145) | | |
| E (p. 145) | | |
| F (p. 145) | | |
| G (p. 145) | | |

Which is the strongest viewpoint? Why do you think so?

## LESSON 28　　What Are the Causes and Effects of More Women Working Outside the Home?

 **Part I**

A higher percentage of women are working outside the home today in the United States than ever before. List below all the causes you can think of for this change.

Now list all the effects of more women working outside the home.

 **Part II**

Read each of the arguments below, then answer the questions. The tables referred to in the questions begin on page 155.

---

### Historian A

Today (1979) more women are working outside the home than ever before, and the divorce rate has never been higher. Obviously, women going off to work is a big factor in the breakup of marriages.

---

1. Which table shows that more women were working in 1979 than ever before?

*[Continued on next page.]*

---

*[Continued from previous page,]*

2. Which table shows that the divorce rate was higher in 1979 than ever before?

3. Identify the primary type of reasoning used in this argument (cause-and-effect, comparison, generalization, proof-by-authority, etc.).

4. What fallacy does this argument commit? (See pp. 6–14 in the "Guide to Critical Thinking," Unit 1. )

5. What is needed to make this argument stronger?

## Historian B

   As women have had fewer children, more women have joined the labor force. Thus, smaller families have allowed women to work more.

6. Which table shows that women have had fewer children?

7. What is the primary type of reasoning used in this argument?

8. Evaluate this argument.

*[Continued on next page.]*

*[Continued from previous page.]*

## Historian C

Though more women are involved in the labor force, they still have not achieved equality with men in the workplace.

9.  Which table is related to this argument?

10. Does this related table support or weaken the argument? Why do you think so?

## Historian D

The biggest factor contributing to the significantly lower earnings of women, compared to those of men, is discrimination. Women are simply not allowed into the top executive and professional positions in the same numbers as men.

11. Does Table 4 support or weaken this argument?

12. If women live longer than men, why do they work only about half the years men work? Write as many reasons as you can think of.

13. Why, according to Table 4, might women get lower pay?

*[Continued on next page.]*

*[Continued from previous page.]*

**Table I**   The Female Labor Force

| Year | Female Labor Force as Percentage of Total Labor Force | Female Labor Force as Percentage of Female Population | |
|------|--------|--------|--------|
| | | **Total** | **Married** |
| 1890 | 16 | 18 | 5 |
| 1900 | 18 | 20 | 6 |
| 1910 | 21 | 24 | 11 |
| 1920 | 20 | 23 | 9 |
| 1930 | 22 | 24 | 12 |
| 1940 | 25 | 27 | 17 |
| 1950 | 29 | 31 | 25 |
| 1960 | 33 | 35 | 32 |
| 1970 | 38 | 43 | 41 |
| 1974 | 39 | 45 | 44 |

Source: *1975 Handbook of Women Working*, pp. 9–18.

**Table 2**   Women's Earnings as a Percentage of Men's Earnings

| Year | Women's Earnings |
|------|------------------|
| 1955 | 64 |
| 1960 | 61 |
| 1965 | 60 |
| 1970 | 59 |
| 1975 | 59 |
| 1977 | 59 |
| 1978 | 59 |

Source: *Perspectives*, p. 52.

*[Continued on next page.]*

*[Continued from previous page.]*

**Table 3**     Birth, Marriage, and Divorce Rates per 1000 Population

| Year | Births | Marriages | Divorces |
|------|--------|-----------|----------|
| 1910 | 30.1 | 10.3 | 0.9 |
| 1920 | 27.7 | 12.0 | 1.6 |
| 1930 | 21.3 | 9.2 | 1.6 |
| 1940 | 19.4 | 12.1 | 2.0 |
| 1950 | 24.1 | 11.1 | 2.6 |
| 1960 | 23.7 | 8.5 | 2.2 |
| 1970 | 18.4 | 10.6 | 3.5 |
| 1978 | 15.3 | 10.3 | 5.1 |

Source: *Statistical Abstracts of the United States,* 1979, p. 60.

**Table 4**     Life Expectancy[1] and Work-life Expectancy[2] by Date and Sex

| Year | Life | | Work-life | |
|------|------|------|------|------|
|      | F | M | F | M |
| 1900 | 50.7 | 48.2 | 6.3 | 32.1 |
| 1940 | 65.9 | 61.2 | 12.1 | 38.2 |
| 1950 | 71.0 | 65.5 | 15.2 | 41.9 |
| 1960 | 73.1 | 66.6 | 20.1 | 41.4 |
| 1970 | 74.6 | 67.1 | 22.9 | 41.4 |
| 1980 | 77.6 | 70.0 | 29.4 | 38.8 |

[1] Average number of years expected to live.

[2] Average number of years expected to work.

Source: Anne Chapman, ed., *Approaches
to Women's History* (1979), p. 106;
also *Monthly Labor Review, August 1985.*

*[Continued on next page.]*

*[Continued from previous page.]*

 **Part III     New Information**

So far you have made some hypotheses about why women work, what the effects of them working are, and why women receive lower pay than men. Now, suppose you found the information in the tables and graphs below. Study this information, then write new explanations for why more women are working, what the effects are, and why they receive lower pay. Information in the tables was published by the Bureau of Labor Statistics.

A. Why did more women work in 1979 than ever before? Cite particular tables or graphs to support your hypothesis.

B. What are the effects of the increase in the number of working women?

C. Why do women receive lower pay than men?

**Table 5**     Population per Household

| Year | Average Household |
|------|-------------------|
| 1900 | 4.76 |
| 1910 | 4.54 |
| 1920 | 4.34 |
| 1930 | 4.11 |
| 1940 | 3.67 |
| 1950 | 3.37 |
| 1960 | 3.33 |
| 1970 | 3.14 |
| 1978 | 2.81 |

Source: *Household and Family Characteristics*, 1979, p. 2.

*[Continued on next page.]*

*[Continued from previous page.]*

**Table 6**    Occupation of the Experienced Civilian Labor Force

| No. of workers (in 1000s) | 1900 | 1919 | 1920 | 1930 | 1940 | 1950 | 1960 | 1970 |
|---|---|---|---|---|---|---|---|---|
| *Professional & Technical* | | | | | | | | |
| Total (both sexes) | 1234 | 1758 | 2283 | 3311 | 3879 | 5081 | 7335 | 11018 |
| Women | 434 | 726 | 1008 | 1482 | 1608 | 2007 | 2793 | 4398 |
| *Managers* | | | | | | | | |
| Total (both sexes) | 1697 | 2462 | 2803 | 3614 | 3770 | 5155 | 5489 | 6224 |
| Women | 74 | 150 | 191 | 292 | 414 | 700 | 794 | 1034 |
| *Clerical* | | | | | | | | |
| Total (both sexes) | 877 | 1987 | 3385 | 4336 | 4982 | 7232 | 9617 | 13457 |
| Women | 212 | 688 | 1614 | 2246 | 2700 | 4502 | 6497 | 9910 |
| *Sales* | | | | | | | | |
| Total (both sexes) | 1307 | 1755 | 2058 | 3059 | 3450 | 4133 | 4801 | 5433 |
| Women | 228 | 379 | 541 | 736 | 925 | 1418 | 1746 | 2097 |
| *Manual* | | | | | | | | |
| Total (both sexes) | 10401 | 14234 | 16974 | 19272 | 20597 | 24266 | 25617 | 27358 |
| Women | 1477 | 1914 | 2052 | 2134 | 2720 | 3685 | 4006 | 5041 |
| *Service* | | | | | | | | |
| Total (both sexes) | 2626 | 3562 | 3313 | 4772 | 6069 | 6180 | 7590 | 9195 |
| Women | 1886 | 2413 | 2063 | 2954 | 3699 | 3532 | 4780 | 5752 |
| *Farm* | | | | | | | | |
| Total (both sexes) | 10888 | 11533 | 11390 | 10321 | 8995 | 6953 | 4085 | 2345 |
| Women | 1008 | 1175 | 1169 | 908 | 508 | 601 | 390 | 222 |

Source: *Historical Statistics of the United States, Colonial Times to 1970* (1976), pp. 139–40.

**Table 7**    Percent of Wives in the Labor Force with Children under 18

| Year | % |
|---|---|
| 1950 | 18.4% |
| 1955 | 24.0 |
| 1960 | 27.6 |
| 1965 | 32.2 |
| 1970 | 39.7 |
| 1975 | 44.9 |
| 1979 | 51.9 |

Source: *Perspectives on Working Women* (1980), p. 27.

*[Continued on next page.]*

*[Continued from previous page.]*

**Table 8**    Marital Status of Women in the Civilian Labor Force: 1960–1980

| Year | Percent Distribution, Female Labor Force | | | Female Labor Force as Percent of Female Population | | | | |
|------|--------|---------|---------------------|-------|--------|--------|-----------------|---------------------|
|      | Single | Married | Widowed or Divorced | Total | Single | Married | | Widowed or Divorced |
|      |        |         |                     |       |        | Total | Husband Present |                     |
| 1960 | 24.0% | 59.9% | 16.1% | 34.8% | 44.1% | 31.7% | 30.5% | 37.1% |
| 1965 | 22.8 | 62.2 | 15.0 | 36.7 | 40.5 | 35.7 | 34.7 | 35.7 |
| 1970 | 22.3 | 63.4 | 14.3 | 42.6 | 53.0 | 41.4 | 40.8 | 36.2 |
| 1971 | 22.7 | 63.0 | 14.2 | 42.5 | 52.8 | 41.4 | 40.8 | 35.7 |
| 1972 | 22.8 | 62.9 | 14.3 | 43.7 | 55.0 | 42.2 | 41.5 | 37.2 |
| 1973 | 22.9 | 62.8 | 14.2 | 44.2 | 55.9 | 42.8 | 42.2 | 36.7 |
| 1974 | 23.4 | 62.2 | 14.4 | 45.3 | 57.4 | 43.8 | 43.1 | 37.8 |
| 1975 | 23.2 | 62.3 | 14.5 | 46.0 | 57.0 | 45.1 | 44.4 | 37.7 |
| 1976 | 24.2 | 61.6 | 14.3 | 46.8 | 59.2 | 45.8 | 45.1 | 37.3 |
| 1977 | 24.2 | 61.0 | 14.8 | 48.0 | 59.2 | 47.2 | 46.6 | 39.0 |
| 1978 | 25.1 | 59.8 | 15.1 | 49.2 | 60.7 | 48.1 | 47.5 | 39.9 |
| 1979 | 25.8 | 59.5 | 14.8 | 50.8 | 62.9 | 49.9 | 49.3 | 40.0 |
| 1980 | 25.0 | 59.7 | 15.3 | 51.1 | 61.5 | 50.7 | 50.1 | 41.0 |

Source: Bulletin 2307

**Graph 9**    Hours Per Week Devoted to Household Work

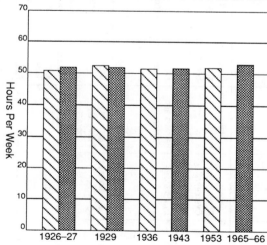

Note:    Slanted column is hours for rural women, solid column is hours for urban women. Chart on the basis of surveys made in the years cited for women with no outside employment. Technological changes have increased women's productivity and shortened the hours necessary to do certain tasks (i.e., laundry), but the addition of new tasks and the creation of higher standards of cleanliness has meant that the hours necessary for housework have not noticeably changed.

Joann Vanek, "Time Spent in Housework," *Scientific American*, November 1974, p. 118.

*[Continued on next page.]*

*[Continued from previous page.]*

## Table 10   The Leading 10 Occupations of Women Workers 1870-1970

In order of size, and as reported in each census regardless of changes in definition.

| | 1870 | 1880 | 1890 | 1900 | 1910 | 1920 | 1930 | 1940 | 1950 | 1960 | 1970 |
|---|---|---|---|---|---|---|---|---|---|---|---|
| 1 | Domestic Servants | Domestic Servants | Servants | Servants | Other Servants | Other Servants | Other Servants, Other Domestic and Personal Service | Servants (private family) | Stenographers, Typists and Secretaries | Stenographers, Typists and Secretaries | Secretaries |
| 2 | Agricultural Laborers | Agricultural Laborers | Agricultural Laborers | Farm Laborers (members of family) | Farm Laborers (home farm) | Teachers (school) | Teachers (school) | Stenographers, Typists and Secretaries | Other Clerical Workers | Other Clerical Workers | Sales Clerks (retail trade) |
| 3 | Tailoresses and Seamstresses | Milliners, Dressmakers and Seamstresses | Dressmakers | Dressmakers | Laundresses (not in Laundry) | Farm Laborers (home farm) | Stenographers and Typists | Teachers (not elsewhere classified) | Saleswomen | Private Household Workers | Bookkeepers |
| 4 | Milliners, Dress and Mantua Makers | Teachers and Scientific Persons | Teachers | Teachers | Teachers (school) | Stenographers and Typists | Other Clerks (except clerks in stores) | Clerical and Kindred Workers (not elsewhere classified) | Private Household Workers | Saleswoman | Teachers (elementary school) |
| 5 | Teachers (not specified) | Laundresses | Farmers, Planters and Overseers | Laundry Work (hand) | Dressmakers and Seamstresses (not in factory) | Other Clerks (except clerks in stores) | Saleswoman | Saleswoman (not elsewhere classified) | Teachers (elementary school) | Teachers (elementary school) | Typists |
| 6 | Cotton-mill Operatives | Cotton-mill Operatives | Cotton-mill Operatives | Farmers and Planters | Farm Laborers (working out) | Laundresses (not in laundry) | Farm Laborers (unpaid family workers) | Operatives and Kindred Workers, Apparel and Accessories | Waitresses | Bookkeepers | Waitresses |
| 7 | Laundresses | Farmers and Planters | Seamstresses | Farm and Plantation Laborers | Cooks | Saleswomen (stores) | Bookkeepers and Cashiers | Bookkeepers, Accountants and Cashiers | Bookkeepers | Waitresses | Sewers and Stitchers |
| 8 | Woolen-mill Operatives | Tailoresses | Cotton-mill Operatives | Saleswomen | Stenographers and Typewriters | Bookkeepers and Cashiers | Laundresses (not in laundry) | Waitresses (except private family) | Sewers and Stitchers, Manufacturing | Miscellaneous and Not Specified Operatives | Nurses, Registered |
| 9 | Farmers and Planters | Woolen-mill Operatives | Housekeepers and Stewards | Housekeepers and Stewards | Farmers | Cooks | Trained Nurses | Housekeepers (private family) | Nurses, Registered | Nurses, Registered | Cashiers |
| 10 | Nurses | Employees of Hotels and Restaurants (not clerks) | Clerks and Copyists | Seamstresses | Saleswomen (stores) | Farmers (general farms) | Other Cooks | Trained Nurses and Student Nurses | Telephone Operators | Other Service Workers (except private household) | Private Household Cleaners and Servants |

*Sources: Decennial Census, 1870-1940; Janet M. Hooks, Women's Occupations Through Seven Decades (Women's Bureau Bulletin #218, U.S. Department of Labor); U.S. Dept. of Commerce, Bureau of the Census: Census of Population, 1960, Detailed Characteristics, U.S. Summary, Table 202; U.S. Department of Commerce, Bureau of the Census: Census of Population, 1970, Detailed Characteristics, U.S. Summary, PC (1)D1; U.S. Women's Bureau, "Occupations of Women, 1950, 1960 and 1970, Tables Reprinted from the Economic Report of the President 1973," 1973.*

# LESSON 29    Was the Kennedy Assassination a Conspiracy?

## Background Information

On November 22, 1963, the American public was shocked by the assassination of one of its most beloved presidents, John F. Kennedy. Lee Harvey Oswald was arrested for the assassination. But two days later, as he was being taken from the Dallas Police Station, Oswald was, in turn, murdered by Jack Ruby, leaving many unanswered questions.

The Warren Commission studied the assassination and concluded in 1964 that Oswald acted alone. Nevertheless, some historians argue that the assassination was a conspiracy (carried out by more than one gunman). This lesson presents two viewpoints on this controversy.

Before the viewpoints is a diagram showing Dealey Plaza in Dallas, where the assassination took place. Included in the diagram are the location of the book depository, where Oswald allegedly fired at the President; the grassy knoll, where some writers believe there was a second assassin; the location of Abraham Zapruder, who was recording the presidential motorcade with his own movie camera for his employees; and locations of several other eyewitnesses.

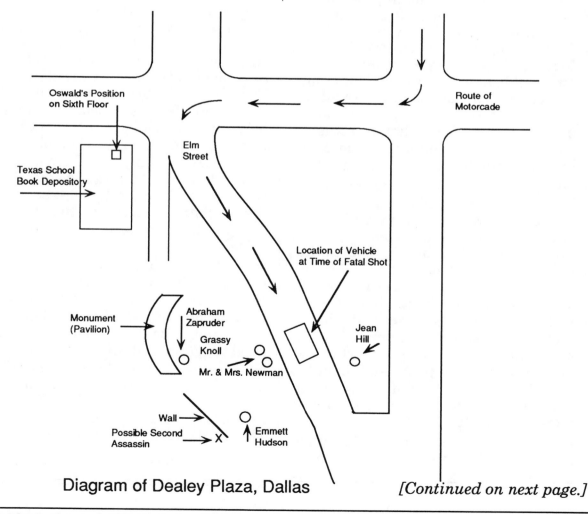

Diagram of Dealey Plaza, Dallas                    *[Continued on next page.]*

*[Continued from previous page.]*

## Interpretation A

*(1)* The assassination of President John F. Kennedy on November 22, 1963, was one of the great tragedies in American history. The country lost one of its best presidents on that day in Dallas. As the country mourned, the question of a conspiracy emerged. The Warren Commission tried to settle the question by concluding that Lee Harvey Oswald had acted alone. But questions remain, and as the evidence has piled up, it has become more certain that Oswald did not act alone. The assassination was carried out by at least two gunmen who were part of a conspiracy to kill the President.

*(2)* Two groups had a motive for killing Kennedy. The Cuban government under the Communist Fidel Castro may have wanted revenge on the President for the attempt to overthrow Castro in the 1961 Bay of Pigs invasion, and also for a plot to assassinate the Communist leader, which had been approved by Robert Kennedy, the president's brother. Castro said that if an agent was hired to kill him, then he could hire someone to kill the President.[1]

*(3)* The Mafia was very upset with the Kennedys for their blacklist consisting of the most wanted mobsters.[2] The anticrime actions of the Kennedys had made things difficult for the Mafia. Labor leader Jimmy Hoffa, who had connections to organized crime, was at the top of the blacklist. He expressed violent hatred for the Kennedy family and wanted all of them dead.[3] It is interesting that Jack Ruby, who was known to have ties to the Mafia,[4] killed Oswald only two days after the assassination, making a conspiracy much more difficult to discover.

*(4)* Other evidence supports the claim that one of these two groups may have been involved in the assassination. Sylvia Odio was visited at her home in Dallas in September 1963 by two Cubans and an American. One of the Cubans said the American was so crazy, "He might even shoot the President...."[5] She later identified the American as Lee Harvey Oswald. Why was Oswald with Cubans? On November 20, 1963, Jack Ruby's waitress, Rose Sharime, overheard Jack Ruby and Lee Harvey Oswald talking about assassinating President Kennedy. Sharime was later thrown from a car and hospitalized.[6]

*(5)* The physical evidence and eyewitness accounts of the assassination make it clear that Oswald could not have acted alone. The eyewitnesses say they heard three shots, two of which were less than a second apart.[7] It would have taken Oswald about 3 to 4 seconds between shots, so he could not have fired all the shots people heard. The film taken by Abraham Zapruder also supports this conclusion. In the film, one can note the moments when Kennedy and Governor Connolly were shot. They are only two frames apart and each frame is 1/18th of a second.[8] So Kennedy and Connolly were shot less than a quarter of a second apart, much too fast for one gunman to fire two shots.

*(6)* The Zapruder film also showed that Oswald could not have fired three shots in the time between his first clear view of the car and when the last shot was fired. The Warren Commission tried to get around this timing problem by saying that the first shot, fired before Oswald had a clear view, missed everything. The second bullet hit Kennedy in the throat and then hit Connolly. The third one hit Kennedy in the head.

*[Continued on next page.]*

## Interpretation A

*[Continued from previous page.]*

**(7)** The second "magic" bullet appeared mysteriously on the stretcher when Connolly was being transferred. The doctor involved feels it may have been "planted" (put there to mislead people) on the stretcher. This bullet was supposed to have gone through Kennedy's throat, entering Connolly's back and shattering one of his ribs, continuing through his arm striking the radial bone, and ending with a fragment entering his right thigh. All this and the bullet was basically undamaged! Later tests, shooting the same type of bullet through goat ribs and a radial bone, show that the bullet would have been much more flattened and have had substantial damage.[9] Moreover, Kennedy and Connolly were not in a straight line, so the bullet would have had to change directions. This evidence shows that more than one bullet hit Kennedy and Connolly, which means more than one assassin.

**(8)** A great deal of evidence indicates that the second assassin fired from the grassy knoll in front and to the right of the President (see the diagram on p. 161). First, the Zapruder film shows the President's head snapping backwards when the fatal shot hit.[10] If he had been hit by Oswald's shot from directly behind him, his head would have gone forward. This is confirmed by a test of shooting a human skull from behind with a high powered rifle—the skull was projected forward.[11]

**(9)** Second, most of the eyewitnesses said they heard the shots from the direction of the grassy knoll and saw a puff of smoke on the knoll.[12] Jean Hill not only saw a gunman in the bushes on the grassy knoll, she chased him. The Warren Commission said he never existed. Hill was threatened by Warren Commission officials, the FBI, and the secret service when she tried to tell her story.[13] Phil Willis took photographs of the motorcade and, in one picture, there is the shape of a man at the end of the wall on the grassy knoll.[14] When authorities checked the area of the grassy knoll where the gunman was suspected to be, they found fresh footprints and smoking cigarette butts.[15]

**(10)** When doctors first examined the body at Dallas Hospital, one doctor concluded that the wound on Kennedy's head was an entrance wound, showing the shot had come from the grassy knoll. When the body arrived at Bethesda Hospital, a new bullet wound appeared, apparently an entrance wound from the rear, pointing to Oswald as the lone killer. The plane arrived a half hour late. The new wound could have been made by surgery.

**(11)** It is clear that Lee Harvey Oswald did not act alone in assassinating President Kennedy. The evidence points to a second assassin on the grassy knoll. Right after the assassination, evidence was planted and altered to cover up the conspiracy, and then Oswald himself was silenced. But the evidence can be pieced together to reconstruct what really happened.

### Endnotes for Interpretation A
[1] Reg Gadney, "Kennedy," NBC, November 19, 1988.
[2] Jack Anderson, "American Expose: Who Murdered JFK?" CBS, November 8, 1988.
[3] Ibid.

*[Continued on next page.]*

## *Endnotes for Interpretation A*
*[Continued from previous page.]*

[4] David W. Berlin, *November 22, 1963: You Are the Jury*. (New York: New York Times Book Co.), p. 92.

[5] Michael Kurtz, *Crime of the Century: Assassination from a Historian's Perspective*. (Nashville, TN: University of Tennessee Press), p. 219. This statement was made by the Cuban named Leopoldo.

[6] Anderson.

[7] Mark Lane, *Rush to Judgment*. (New York; Fawcett World Library, 1966) p. 143.

[8] Robert Richter, "Who Shot President Kennedy?" ABC, November 15, 1988.

[9] Ibid. The results of the test were stated by the congressional committee studying the assassination.

[10] Ibid.

[11] Ibid. A pathologist explained these results.

[12] Lane, pp. 140, 261; David Lifton, *Best Evidence*. (New York: Macmillan, 1980) p. 16. Jean Hill said she thought the shots came from across the street "from the knoll" (see the diagram). Mr. & Mrs. Newman (diagram) said the shots came from directly behind them. Emmett Hudson (diagram) said the shots came from directly over his head. Sam Holland said he saw a puff of smoke come from behind the arcade and through the trees. Johnson testified that white smoke was observed near the pavilion. And there were numerous others with similar testimony.

[13] "Story of a Second Gunman Was Never Explored, Says Witness." *Boston Herald*, November 20, 1988, p. 7.

[14] Lifton, photographs after p. 44; NOVA, "Who Shot President Kennedy," narrated by Walter Cronkite, WGBH, November 15, 1988.

[15] NOVA.

[16] Lifton, p. 87.

## Interpretation B

(1) The assassination of President John F. Kennedy brought great sorrow to our nation. The leader who had inspired such great hopes was suddenly gone. The loss was intense. The public was bewildered. Out of our agony a new question emerged. Had Lee Harvey Oswald acted alone or was the assassination a conspiracy? Despite the Warren Commission's conclusions that Oswald was the lone assassin, conspiracy theories continue to emerge, born of fertile imaginations rather than adherence to the evidence.

(2) The Mafia and the Cubans supposedly had motives to kill President Kennedy. A lot of people had a motive to kill him, so that doesn't mean much. There are coincidences of meetings and snippets of conversations that sound odd, but no hard evidence of conspiracy. The theory that Jack Ruby killed Oswald for the Mafia, to cover up the conspiracy is, in fact, disproved by the evidence. Oswald was scheduled to leave the Dallas Police Department at 10:00 A.M. Ruby was making a financial transaction at a nearby bank after 11:00 A.M. Unknown to him, Oswald was delayed. Ruby shot Oswald at 11:21 A.M. in what surely was a coincidence, with Ruby walking in at the right time, not planning a "hit" as a Mafia hitman would have.[1]

(3) The physical evidence is overwhelming that Oswald, and he alone, killed the President. Two large bullet fragments found in the limousine, along with the nearly whole bullet found on the stretcher, were analyzed against the three cartridge cases found in the Texas Book Depository by four experts in firearms identification. They determined that Oswald's rifle, to the exclusion of other weapons, fired the bullets that struck President Kennedy and Governor Connolly.[2]

*[Continued on next page.]*

## Interpretation B

*[Continued from previous page.]*

*(4)* The so-called "magic" bullet has caused a great deal of controversy. Physical evidence shows it did come out of Governor Connolly's leg—it was not placed on the stretcher as part of a conspiracy. Testing on the magic bullet, and bullet fragments found in the Governor's leg, show they are chemically identical.[3]

*(5)* Critics have charged, based on the Zapruder film, that the President and the Governor were not lined up so that a bullet (the second bullet) fired from the sixth floor of the Depository could have caused the President's neck wounds and the Governor's chest, wrist and thigh wounds. But the FBI restaged the assassination according to the Zapruder film and concluded the single bullet could, in fact, have inflicted all the wounds if the President was leaning slightly forward and downward, and if Connolly was leaning slightly backward and to the left.[4] These conditions fit perfectly with the position of the two men in the film at the time the Warren Commission claims the second bullet struck.[5] Experts have also done tests shooting bullets through gelatin (which is similar to human flesh) and the bullets tend to change direction, making possible a slight discrepancy in the positioning of President Kennedy and Governor Connolly in the limousine.

*(6)* As for the pristine (relatively undamaged) state of the magic bullet, ballistics evidence shows that a bullet which is slowed down, such as this bullet was after entering Kennedy's body, is less likely to be damaged.[6]

*(7)* Some writers argue that the two wounds on the front of Kennedy's head and neck were entrance wounds, showing that the President was shot from the grassy knoll. They base this claim on the autopsy report from Parkland Hospital in Dallas, in which two wounds were noted. They claim the body was altered on the flight to Bethesda Memorial Hospital where the autopsy noted four wounds, two entrance wounds in the rear of the body. The discrepancy is easily explained. The whole time the body was at Parkland it was on its back,[7] so the doctors did not see the other two wounds.

*(8)* FBI experts who examined the holes in the President's clothing concluded, by the size of the holes and the direction that the fibers had been pushed, that the bullet entered through his back and exited through his neck.[8] Pathologists also testified that the small hole in the back of the President's head was the entrance wound and the large crater was the exit.[9]

*(9)* Four of the doctors who originally examined the President's body at Bethesda recently independently examined the X-rays, never having seen them before. All four concluded that, based on their observations at Bethesda, there were no changes to the wounds from when the photographs and X-rays were taken at Parkland Hospital in Dallas.[10]

*(10)* Another controversial point is that the Zapruder film shows the President's head snap backward at the time of the fatal shot, indicating impact from the front rather than the rear. Experts conducted a test in which they fired a shot into a skull filled with fake brain matter that was set on top of a ladder. They used a rifle similar to Oswald's rifle and the same angle and distance as in the assassination. Despite the rear entrance, the skull was blown back-

*[Continued on next page.]*

## Interpretation B

*[Continued from previous page.]*

wards, just as Kennedy's head had been.[11]

(11) Supporters of the conspiracy theory believe that the second assassin was on the grassy knoll. They make a great deal out of the footprints and cigarette butts in the area. This just means someone was watching the motorcade, not that a murderer was there. The photographs of the grassy knoll containing shapes, possibly of a man or men, are also not conclusive. Experts who examined the photographs and electronically enhanced them said that some of the shapes could be human, but it takes a lot of imagination to conclude that they are human.[12]

(12) All of the evidence compiled by the Warren Commission was hard evidence and its conclusion that Lee Harvey Oswald, acting alone, assassinated President Kennedy is still the soundest conclusion yet reached. The mystique of conspiracy arose amid the confusion and bewilderment of the witnesses in the hours and days after the dreadful events of November 22, 1963. An eternal flame burns over Kennedy's grave in Arlington National Cemetery and, just as that flame will burn forever, so will the flame of conspiracy.

### *Endnotes for Interpretation B*

[1] David W. Belin, "The Warren Commission—Why We Still Don't Believe It," *The New York Times Magazine*, November 20, 1988, p. 76.

[2] *Report of the Warren Commission on the Assassination of President Kennedy*, (New York: McGraw Hill, 1964), pp. 88–89.

[3] NOVA, "Who Shot President Kennedy?" narrated by Walter Cronkite, WGBH, November 15, 1988.

[4] Ibid.

[5] Ibid.

[6] Ibid.

[7] Warren Commission, pp. 91–95.

[8] Ibid.

[9] Ibid.

[10] NOVA.

[11] Ibid.

[12] Ibid.

# Major Sources Used for Lessons

## Lesson 6

Bailey, Thomas A. *A Diplomatic History of the American People*. New York: Meredith Corporation, 8th edition, 1969, Chapter 31 "The Coming of the War with Spain, 1895–1898."

Beisner, Robert. *From the Old Diplomacy to the New, 1865–1900*. Arlington Heights, IL: AHM Publishing, 1975, Chapter 5 "War, Policy, and Imperialism at the End of the Century, 1897–1900."

## Lesson 7

Julien, Claude. *America's Empire*. New York: Random House, 1971, Chapter II "The Birth of Imperialism."

Lebergott, Stanley. "The Returns to U.S. Imperialism, 1890–1929." *The Journal of Economic History*, Vol. XL, June 1980, pp. 229–52.

Lenin, V.I. *Imperialism, the Highest Stage of Capitalism: A Popular Outline*. New York: China Books, 1939.

## Lesson 8

Bailey, Thomas A. and Paul B. Ryan. *The Lusitania Disaster*. New York: Macmillan, 1975.

Simpson, Colin. *The Lusitania*. Boston: Little Brown, 1972.

## Lesson 9

Cramer, Kenyon C. *The Causes of War*. Glenview, IL: Scott, Foresman, 1965, pp. 124–26 on the Nye Committee Report.

Link, Arthur. *Woodrow Wilson and the Progressive Era*. New York: Harper and Row, 1954, pp. 275–81.

Peterson, H.C. *Propaganda for War*. Norman, OK: University of Oklahoma Press, 1934, pp. 327–30.

Seymour, Charles. *American Neutrality, 1914–1917*. New Haven: Yale University Press, 1935, pp. 1–11, 168–71.

## Lesson 10

Cummins, D. Duane and William Gee White, *Contrasting Decades: The 1920's and 1930's*. New York: Benziger, 1972, Chapter 5 "The New Deal."

## Lesson 12

Mowry, George E., ed. *Fords, Flappers and Fanatics*. Englewood Cliffs, NJ: Prentice-Hall, 1963.

## Lesson 13

Feuerlicht, Roberta S. *Justice Crucified: The Story of Sacco and Vanzetti*. New York: McGraw-Hill, 1977.

Krug, Madeleine. "Sacco and Vanzetti: Guilty as Charged?" Wilton, CT: Current Affairs Films, 1977.

Russell, Francis. *Tragedy in Dedham: The Story of the Sacco-Vanzetti Case*. New York: McGraw-Hill, 1962.

"Sacco-Vanzetti Student Renders His Final Verdict," *Boston Globe*, April 13, 1986, pp. B–13, 14.

## Lesson 14

Brownlee, W. Elliott. *Dynamics of Ascent: A History of the American Economy*. New York: Alfred A. Knopf, 1974.

Friedman, Milton and Anna Schwartz. *The Great Contraction: 1920–1933*. Princeton, NJ: Princeton University Press, 1965.

Kindleberger, Charles. *Manias, Panics, and Crashes: A History of Financial Crisis*. New York: Basic Books, 1978.

Rose, Stephen and Steven Miller. "The Great Depression: A Study of Misinformation in Secondary American History Textbooks." Paper presented at the Northeast Regional Conference for the Social Studies, March, 1982.

Temin, Peter. *Did Monetary Forces Cause the Great Depression?* New York: Norton, 1976.

## Lesson 16

Conkin, Paul K. *The New Deal*. New York: Crowell, 1967.

Gruver, Rebecca Brooks. *An American History*. Reading, MA: Addison-Wesley, 1976 "Interpreting the New Deal," pp. 851–52.

Leuchtenburg, William E. *Franklin D. Roosevelt and the New Deal, 1932–1940*. New York: Harper and Row, 1963.

## Lesson 20

Alperovitz, Gar. *Atomic Diplomacy: Hiroshima and Potsdam*. New York: Simon and Schuster, 1965.

Butow, Robert J.C. *Japan's Decision to Surrender*. Stanford: Stanford University Press, 1954.

Feis, Herbert. *The Atomic Bomb and the End of World War II*. Princeton, NJ: Princeton University Press, 1966.

*Foreign Relations Papers of the United States: the Potsdam Conference, 1945*. Washington, DC: Government Printing Office.

©1991 Midwest Publications/Critical Thinking Press and Software, P.O. Box 448, Pacific Grove, CA 93950

"Ike on Ike," *Newsweek*, November 11, 1963.

Stimson, Henry L. "The Decision to Use the Atomic Bomb," *Harper's*, February, 1947, pp. 97–107.

## Lesson 21

Bernstein, Barton J. "American Foreign Policy and the Origins of the Cold War" in Barton J. Bernstein, ed. *Politics and Policies of the Truman Administration*. Chicago: Quadrangle, 1970.

Brzezinski, Zbigniew K. *The Soviet Bloc*. Cambridge, MA: Harvard University Press, 1967.

*Foreign Relations Papers of the United States*, 1943, 1944, 1945, 1946, The Conferences at Malta and Yalta, and the Potsdam Conference. Washington, DC: Government Printing Office.

Gaddis, John Lewis. *The United States and the Origins of the Cold War, 1941–1947*. New York: Columbia University Press, 1972.

Herz, Martin. *Beginnings of the Cold War*. New York: McGraw-Hill, 1966.

Kolko, Gabriel and Joyce Kolko. *The Limits of Power: The World and United States Foreign Policy, 1945–1954*. New York: Harper and Row, 1972.

La Feber, Walter. *America, Russia and the Cold War: 1945–1971*. New York: Wiley, 1972.

Mark, Eduard. "American Policy toward Eastern Europe and the Origins of the Cold War, 1941–1946: An Alternative Explanation." *Journal of American History*, Vol. 68: September, 1981, pp. 313–36.

McNeill, William H. *America, Britain and Russia, Their Cooperation and Conflict, 1941–1946*. New York: Oxford University Press, 1953.

Schlesinger, Arthur M., Jr. "Origins of the Cold War," *Foreign Affairs*, Vol. 47: October, 1961, pp. 22–51.

Truman, Harry S. *The Presidential Memoirs of Harry S. Truman, Year of Decisions*, Volume I. New York: Doubleday, 1955.

Williams, William A. *The Tragedy of American Diplomacy*. New York: Dell Publishing Co., 1959.

## Lesson 22

Fitzgerald, Frances. *Fire in the Lake: The Vietnamese and the Americans in Vietnam*. New York: Random House, 1972.

Halberstam, David. *The Best and the Brightest*. New York: Fawcett World, 1973.

Kahin, George McTurnan and John W. Lewis. *The United States in Vietnam*. New York: Dell Publishing Co., 1969.

Lewy, Guenter. *America in Vietnam*. New York: Oxford University Press, 1978.

Littauer, Raphael and Norman Uphoff, eds. *The Air War in Indochina*. Boston: Beacon Press, 1972.

Pike, Douglas. "The Other Side," *The Wilson Quarterly*, Vol. VII, No. 3, Summer, 1983, pp. 120–28.

Pike, Douglas. *Viet Cong: The Organization and Techniques of the National Liberation Front of South Vietnam*. Cambridge, MA: MIT Press, 1966.

Thompson, Sir Robert. *No Exit from Vietnam*. New York: David McKay, 1969.

Westmoreland, William C. *A Soldier Reports*. Garden City, NY: Doubleday, 1976.

## Lesson 23

Rovere, Richard H. *Senator Joe McCarthy*. New York: World, 1959.

Steele, Robert V. *When Even Angels Wept: The Senator Joseph McCarthy Affair*. New York: Morrow, 1973.

## Lesson 26

Dollar, Charles M. and Gary Reichard. *American Issues: A Documentary Reader*. New York: Random House, 1988. Chapter 26, Problem 3 "Desegregation and the Southern Reaction."

## Lesson 27

Thernstrom, Stephen. *The Other Bostonians; Poverty and Progress in the American Metropolis, 1880–1970*. Cambridge, MA: Harvard University Press, 1973.

## Lesson 28

Baxandall, Rosalyn, Linda Gordon and Susan Reverby. *America's Working Women: A Documentary History, 1600 to the Present*. New York: Random House, 1976.

Chapman, Anne. "Working with Quantified History: Women in the Labor Force" in Matthew Downey, ed. *Teaching American History*. Washington, DC: National Council for the Social Studies, Bulletin Number 67, 1982, pp. 19–23.

*Statistical Abstract of the United States, 1989*. United States Department of Commerce, Bureau of the Census. Washington, DC: United States Government Printing Office, 1989.

## Lesson 29

Lane, Mark. *Rush to Judgment*. New York: Fawcett, 1966.

Lifton, David S. *Best Evidence*. New York: Macmillan, 1980.

*Report of the Warren Commission on the Assassination of President Kennedy*. New York: McGraw-Hill, 1964.

NOVA. "Who Shot President Kennedy?" Boston: WGBH, November 15, 1988.

 ©1991 MIDWEST PUBLICATIONS/CRITICAL THINKING PRESS AND SOFTWARE, P.O. BOX 448, PACIFIC GROVE, CA 93950